Essays on the History of Bermuda

Dr. Edward Harris, MBE, JP, FSA

VOLUME 1, 2007

Originally published in *The Mid-Ocean News*

BERMUDA MARITIME MUSEUM PRESS

IN MEMORIAM

John Armitage Carstairs Arnell, PhD
1918–2000

*First Chairman of the
Bermuda Maritime Museum*

Ethel Cecilia Campbell Arnell
1913–2006

Friends and colleagues

Heritage Matters, Essays on Bermuda History, Edward Cecil Harris, MBE, JP, PhD, FSA, Executive Director, Bermuda Maritime Museum; Visiting Professor of Anthropology, The College of William & Mary, Virginia. ■ Book and cover designed by Paul Shapiro, Brimstone Media Ltd., Bermuda. ■ Copyright © 2007 Dr. Edward Cecil Harris. ■ Published by the Bermuda Maritime Museum Press, The Keep, Royal Naval Dockyard, Bermuda. ■ No part of this book may be reproduced in any form without the publisher's written permission. ■ Printed in China. ■ ISBN 0–921560–12–5.

Contents

Binding together past and present

Bank of Bermuda Foundation is proud to support community-driven projects that lend cultural, historical and social value to all Bermudians. Our Island's heritage —including arts, culture, history and the environment—has been an important focus of the Foundation's efforts. Over the years, our charitable giving programme has made possible many dynamic initiatives that celebrate Bermuda for the long-term benefit of us all.

This special publication, an anthology of heritage-inspired writings by Dr. Edward Harris, Executive Director of the Bermuda Maritime Museum, fulfills that mandate. The essays, originally published as his weekly column in *The Mid-Ocean News*, have explored fascinating and widely unknown corners of the Island's remarkable heritage— from the role of archaeology and cultural tourism, to maritime exploits and military milestones and to the stories behind long-forgotten monuments of our rich past. The misnomer of "Spanish" Rock, the legacy of limestone, the legend of Venturilla, the loss of built-heritage in the form of simple icons like bus stops or watch houses—these are some of the intriguing topics examined by Dr. Harris, as he binds past and present together, bringing the often esoteric world of history to life in a very readable style. Highly popular with readers of his column over the past two years, his detail-packed writings now come together in a collector's edition that will be treasured by historians and the public alike.

We welcome this compelling addition to the Island's heritage literature, and hope it encourages further understanding, debate and education—as well as community commitment to the preservation of so many facets of Bermuda's unique history.

Joseph C. H. Johnson
Chairman, Bank of Bermuda Foundation

Celebrating our shared history

We increasingly inhabit a present-tense world. It's the sort of live-for-the-moment environment someone once decried as "a culture of impermanence," one in which our long-term memory banks are erased on an almost daily basis and our shared history is subject to the sort of collective amnesia which results in Bermudians forgetting their longstanding commonalities have often far outnumbered their differences.

In this amnesiac culture even the phrase "You're history!" has entered the vernacular as a popular term of abuse, an implicit rebuke to all those who dwell on—and in—the past in order to understand the forces, circumstances and conditions that provided the context for our historical development, shaped our present and signpost the way to our future.

The historian's role, never easy at the best of times, becomes all the more difficult given such adverse circumstances, in which the day-to-day loose change of Bermudian affairs is often assigned a far higher value than the almost 500-year-old treasure trove that is the story of this island's role in human affairs.

The Bermuda Maritime Museum's Executive Director Dr. Edward Harris has been providing weekly reminders of this fascinating story in his ongoing *Mid-Ocean News* series, "Heritage Matters." As you will discover in these articles—which succeed in both stimulating and educating—Dr. Harris has his finger firmly placed on Bermuda's cultural pulse. In these finely written pieces he should convince even those who live in the present to the almost total exclusion of the past they need to begin sparing a thought for a shared history that should not be allowed to become the exclusive preserve of a community of scholars—but rather should belong to the community as a whole.

Tim Hodgson
Editor, *The Mid-Ocean News*

Putting the case for Casemate Barracks

View of the Dockyard including Commissioner's House and the Clocktower Building, from the roof of Casemate Barracks

The Casemate Barracks, one of the most important historic buildings of the Dockyard, has again appeared in the news in an article in *The Mid-Ocean News*. One need not itemise all the mistakes in that story, but it must be pointed out that Casemate Barracks was not built in 1910, but in the 1830s. After the fortifications of the Dockyard, themselves monumental works of three decades from 1809 onwards, and the great Commissioner's House, Casemate Barracks is the oldest standing building of the Bermuda Dockyard.

We now know that all the buildings of the main yard below the barracks were constructed between 1847 and 1857, thanks to a painting in the Fay & Geoffrey Elliott Collection executed in 1847 from the veranda of the Commissioner's House. In this view, there stand only two of the original buildings of the wooden Dockyard, the fortifications and the Casemate Barracks. The yard is a flat, white wasteland created by the blasting away of its hard limestone, to give slaves (until 1834), free men and jailbirds from England (until 1863) the raw material from which they labouriously shaped each and every rock that made up the fortifications, the Barracks and the Commissioner's House.

After 1847, the stone for the Clocktower Building, formerly and gracefully know as the "Great Eastern Storehouse," and the other buildings of the yard was quarried from the area now called the Moresby Playing Fields. All of that rock had to be blasted out of the ground, broken into smaller pieces, which were then chiselled into the stone blocks that account for the grandeur of the Dockyard buildings today. These buildings and the Dockyard fortifications should be added to Bermuda's World Heritage Site inventory.

Casemate Barracks was so named for it was a hostel for the men of the Royal Marine Light Infantry, who were responsible for the defence of the Dockyard, and because its roof, being vaulted in brick and concrete some eight feet thick, was built to make it bomb-proof against the incoming cannon balls and mortar shot of the day. By 1900, such an architectural defence mechanism was obsolete and the building would have been demolished with a couple of rounds of high explosive shells from any cruiser of the US Navy, then the potential enemy.

Casemate Barracks had two floors with accommodation for 120 officers and men, along with canteens, messes and offices. The well that forms the roof has unparalleled views of the Dockyard to the northeast and the building, given its construction, could have been converted into a fort—Bermuda's Alamo, if you will. The walls are several feet thick and being made of the indurated local limestone needed no plastering to make them waterproof. A veranda was to be had on three sides of the building at the level of the ground floor and no doubt many a drink was consumed in that outstanding setting overlooking the Dockyard and the Commissioner's House in the distance. Legend has it that one drunk left the bar there and climbed

EDWARD HARRIS

Then and now: Casemates Barracks when it housed 120 officers and men; and in 2005, replete with prison-era watchtower and invasive casuarinas

over the wall fronting the Dockyard, only to fall some 30 feet into a cart of soft material that saved his life.

On either side of the Barracks was an ordnance yard and there are still found the magnificent gunpowder storage buildings, or magazines. The one to the southeast later became the bakery of the Dockyard and saw its last use as the visitor's entry block into "Casemates," the prison of late decades, now replaced by the Westgate Correctional Facility.

A group of volunteers under Mr. Chris Addams is attempting to clean up the Casemate Barracks complex and they should be congratulated for their hard work. Much needs to be done, if Casemate Barracks, the third most important building of the Dockyard, is to be saved for posterity.

A new use must be found for the building to ensure its use and survival. My colleague, Dr. Clarence Maxwell, the historian, suggests that it should house the Bermuda Archives, which would bring another historical entity into the Dockyard. In some ways, with all its barracks rooms, or cells, the building is well suited to such a new way of life, but other options may be just as viable.

Perhaps under the military-

minded Chairman of the West End Development Corporation, Lt. Col. David Burch, OBE (MIL), ED, JP, the outstanding work of heritage that is Casemate Barracks may again become a vibrant part of the Dockyard. I would suggest, however, that some unclimbable fencing of a prison-type be erected around the Dockyard, should a bar be re-established on the hopefully restored veranda of Casemate Barracks.

The Upper Ordnance Yard and Casemate Barracks

And the walls came tumbling down...

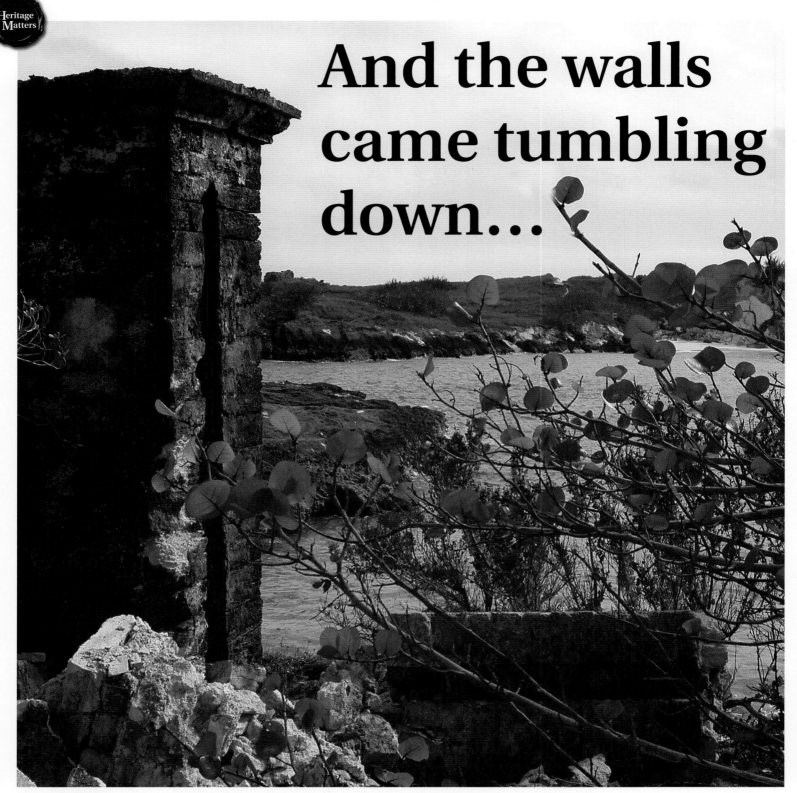

One gate pillar lies in ruins after the onslaught of Hurricane Fabian rolled over historic fortifications at Castle Island

Archaeologists believe that Jericho, where the walls once came tumbling down, is the first city in the world, dating back some 11,000 years. The city where Joshua fit (fought) his battle and destroyed its walls was a later version of Jericho, the epic event taking place some 3,500 years ago, give or take a few hundred years. I was reminded of this story and of a childhood song when viewing the damage to the history fortification that is Castle Island after Hurricane Fabian. The Bible says something different, but whether it was trumpets or a well-timed earthquake, it seems that the defences of Jericho crumbled and Joshua and his army destroyed all the sinners and emblems of decadence within.

Trying to get some more data on Josh and gang, I surfed the Web, only to find almost 400,000 references to the Walls of Jericho and the Walls Tumbling Down. The symbolism of this Biblical story has become an integral part of the modern world and the destruction of the Berlin Wall extending down the middle of Germany some 1,500 miles is but the latest example of this story/song in the context of a fight for liberty.

The song of childhood is of course the spiritual "Joshua Fit the Battle of Jericho," made famous by the outstanding voice of Paul Robeson and adapted by Elvis Presley and many other singers. The University of Denver and its "Spirituals Project" notes: "One important purpose of many spirituals during the slave period was to provide motivation and inspiration for the ongoing struggle for freedom, a

EDWARD HARRIS

Castle Island from the air before Fabian. Inset, the barracks wall knocked flat by Fabian's trumpets

struggle which included systematic efforts to escape from bondage as well as numerous slave-led revolts and insurrections. In the African tradition, stories of ancestors' bravery, victories in battle, and success in overcoming past hardships were often marshalled as inspiration to face current life challenges. As stories of specific African ancestors faded over time, enslaved people appropriated heroes from the Christian Bible as ancestral equivalents. The stories of Old Testament figures—often perceived by enslaved Africans as freedom fighters—held particular significance as models of inspiration."

So it is to that translation of a Bible legend by Africans in America that we probably owe one of the most enduring symbols of the fight for freedom in modern times. The walls I am thinking about, however, were enslaving no one but were captive to the neglect that affects much of our built heritage and to the ravages of the hard blowing trumpets of nature. Castle Island, one of the most important archaeological sites in Bermuda, was devastated by Hurricane Fabian because its defences, literally, had been let down by years of neglect and the encroachment of vegetation.

There is no other site like Castle Island for its time and place and for its survival into present days. Visually, it leaves such sites, like the epochal Jamestown in Virginia, the birthplace of the U.S., in the dust, for nothing remains above ground of that place, started in 1607. No other early English settlement in the Americas can compare with the monuments of Castle Island, for they were built to endure in Bermuda stone, whereas other buildings were of timber and ultimately decayed away. In 1911, in our tradition of producing words without deeds, a law was enacted to protect Castle Island. Others followed later, not to much effect, as Fabian demonstrated.

On this small island are the oldest Bermuda stone house, the King's Castle of 1612, Devonshire Redoubt of 1621 and the Landward Fort, built before 1650. The island has the only 17th century curtain wall in Bermuda, major parts of which Fabian swept into the oblivion of the sea. It also has the oldest masonry toilet of our land, for those of you interested in the fundamentals of life. Castle Island is part of Bermuda's World Heritage Site, high on the list created by UNESCO to mark outstanding monuments of international importance, but it barely registers on the barometers of heritage care in this modern Jericho.

The spiritual goes like this:
Joshua fit de battle ob Jerico / An' de walls come tumblin' down.

The Bible says that when the priests blew with the trumpets the wall fell down flat. At Castle Island, the song gave way to the scripture and the walls were knocked flat. No slowly tumbling down there, but a knockout blow straight to the ground.

Robert Frost, in his poem "The Mending Wall," speaks of two neighbours who live with a stone wall separating them, and "their wall is made of fear and suspicion and misunderstanding as much as it is of stone." One neighbour muses: "Before I built a wall I'd ask to know / What I was walling in or walling out / And to whom I was like to give offence / Something there is that doesn't love a wall / That wants it down."

The walls of Castle Island were made to defend, designed to give offence to our enemies of old. In this day, they offend no one, but delight many as a part of the extraordinary heritage we have inherited from past wall-builders.

There are some who hate such walls, that want them down, that want our history to be a blank slate. We must fight the fight of freedom for these walls, we must rebuilt and preserve, not to offend such Philistines, but in the hope, perhaps forlorn, that they in time might be converted to a love of Bermuda's built heritage.

Robert Frost also wrote that good walls make good neighbours: good walls not only make good heritage, they are essential to its future.

Governor Tucker's illusive Grange

In 1616, when the world was young—four years old—in Bermudian terms, Governor Daniel Tucker descended upon the island, to leave an indelible mark on the place in the shape of many persons who yet bear the family name. Clearly, Daniel Tucker had genes for outstanding self-interest that is nowhere more highly illustrated than in his land dealings in Southampton and Sandys Parish.

At that time, those as yet unnamed lands contained some of the most extensive and fertile farming grounds in Bermuda; the land also had some of the best groundwater deposits in the island. Richard Norwood was then surveying the island for division into plots or shares of 25 and 50 acres, many of the plots running from shore to shore across the land. One of the few—possibly the only— that still bears the name of its owner, is the Hayden Trust area of Somerset, the original property of Bermuda Company shareholder John Hayden. Tucker realised that if he stopped the survey that had progressed into the lower reaches of Southampton, and commanded Norwood to work down from Ireland and Somerset Islands, that there would probably be some extra land available between the two surveyed portions.

That surplus he would arrogate to himself and so it proved, with the "Overplus" in Southampton and Sandys Parishes, falling into his possession. It was on these lands, far from the capital in St. George's, that he would build his outstanding home called The Grange. The building was timber-framed in cedar with wattle and daub infilling and had a mile-long prospect leading to it, possibly from the bay at Far Rockaway. Had The Grange survived, it would undoubtedly be at the top of the register of historic Bermuda houses.

It seems that the building may not have lasted that long, but for a time The Grange was an unparalleled architectural feature of the Bermuda landscape. It was replaced on the same site, or just nearby, by The Grove, built Capt. Henry Tucker around 1720. An outstanding building in itself, The Grove withstood all hurricanes and winds of change until it was demolished in the 1960s. The Grove passed to the Burrows family around 1800 and in 1875 to the Munros, who owned the property until the Port Royal Golf Course was built.

My attention was drawn to The Grange and The Grove by academic colleagues from Williamsburg, Virginia, where a branch of the Tucker family had settled in the 18th century. So one day some

The Grove from an early illustration

Courtesy Nora Kast

It seems that the building may not have lasted that long, but for a time The Grange was an unparalleled architectural feature of the Bermuda landscape

years ago with Kate Meatyard, we went hunting at Port Royal, dodging golf balls and carts, to see if there was any evidence on the surface of these two outstanding Bermudian houses. We found in the pale traces of lighter grass what later proved on excavation to be a cart way for The Grove. Nearby lay a concrete slab, which was covering a well cut into the rock. The dimensions of the well matched that given in archival evidence in *The Rich Papers* and may well, if I may say so, prove to be the one excavated by Daniel Tucker in 1616.

These discoveries led to the mounting of an archaeological project at the site of the houses, through the kind permission of the Trustees of the Port Royal Golf Course. Under the supervision of Dr. Clifford Smith, archaeologist from the Bermuda Maritime Museum, the excavations were led by Professor John Triggs of Wilfrid Laurier University in Waterloo, Ontario.

Professor Triggs brought with him a team of volunteers, including students and professionals in computerised survey work and artifact analysis and several digs of two-weeks duration have now taken place.

In February 2005, the foundations of the southern wall of the main house of The Grove were discovered. Another part of the building was in wood and was found in a deposit of burnt timbers and window glass, overlain by roofing slate. A cartway went past The Grove, probably headed for the farm building to the rear. To the south of the cartway, a pit was located that produced a number of sherds of fine 18th-century pottery, including porcelains, such as one might expect from a prominent family like the Tuckers.

Some 17th-century pottery was found in the lower levels of the excavation, but of the illusive Governor Tucker and his Grange, nothing certain was discovered. The search will continue.

EDWARD HARRIS

Island tomb of the unknown labourers

"**A**dding spiritual insult to fatal injury, we died and were buried on the job building that fort for Bermuda." So might have spoken two unknown labourers working on the rebuilding of Smith's Fort at St. George's in the early 1790s. Scientists from the Bermuda Maritime Museum and the College of William & Mary discovered their earthly remains in 2001, during an otherwise routine archaeological excavation. That dig was undertaken with the blessing of the National Parks Commission.

Smith's Fort was one of the first buildings made of Bermuda stone a year after settlement in late July 1612. The settlers, arriving at what must have looked like paradise on earth after the wet grays of the English climate, were immediately put to work raising fortifications to protect their new establishment from Spanish attack. At the head of the original channel into St. George's Harbour they first erected Paget Fort, within weeks of setting foot on dry land. The following year, Governor Moore had them working at Castle Island, to protect the entrance to Castle Harbour, but then turned his attention to Governor's Island, erecting a gun platform and a redoubt.

The D-shaped gun platform is still visible, but it was the lost redoubt that archaeologists began to look for in 2001. The redoubt was a very small fort in the style of a late Renaissance castle—much like Henry VIII built on the south coast of England some decades before—with two circular towers or bastions and an enclosed courtyard and guardhouse to the rear. This was the only such fort at Bermuda, for all the other early works were built in a fashion to house the new technological wonder, the cannon. Had Smith's Fort survived, it would have been a delightful historic cameo at the entrance of the channel between Paget and St. David's Islands.

That was not to be, for upon losing the east coast of what became the U.S., the British military realised that Bermuda held the key to the defence of the western North Atlantic sea lanes, and the place from where they could control the navy of the new country to the west. At the peace of the American Revolutionary War in 1783, the Royal Engineers—"purveyors of technology to the Empire"—were sent to Bermuda to assess the state of its fortifications and to enhance them for the defence of the island, or more correctly, the protection of a proposed naval station. Bermuda was the only spot between Canada and the West Indies where such a new military emporium could be created. This was lucky for the British and lucky for the Bermudians, who made off like bandits, even then charging exorbitant rents to newcomers and benefiting from the construction of fortifications for the next century and a half.

One of the buildings that was severely altered in the 1790s was Smith's Fort. Captain Andrew Durnford, RE, the first major of St. George's and the author of two large families, one in England and the other out of wedlock here, demolished the 1613 redoubt and replaced it with a bulwark for four large cannon, firing through embrasures or triangular gaps in the masonry. Studying old

Bermudian anthropologist Jenna Judd recording one of the towers of the 1613 Smith's Fort. One of the burials lies to her left (detail inset)

documents, the archaeologists determined the foundations of the towers of the redoubt might be preserved under Durnford's bulwark—and so it proved. The towers were about 10 feet in diameter and very well built in Bermuda stone; very few artifacts were found, suggesting that the fort was not occupied except in emergencies.

Between the gun embrasures were soil and rubble-filled merlons and in two of these, to the astonishment of all, we found two burials, one with an American coin minted in Connecticut in 1787 in the nightshirt pocket in which the body had been laid to rest. A leading forensic anthropologist, Dr. Michael Blakey, at the College of William & Mary where the project archaeologist Dr. Norman Barka also taught, examined the skeletons and both were found to be males. Growths on the collarbones indicated that they were in some type of heavy manual labour, possibly stonecutters, masons or boatmen.

Durnford's surviving records shed no light on labourers having died or being killed on the construction of the fort, so the presence and personages of these two inhumations may forever be a mystery, awaiting cold case archaeological detectives of the future. There were four merlons in Durnford's cannon bulwark and we examined only two. As Prof. Barka once asked, "What would be meant if there are burials in the other two merlons?"

Jervis Bay: against hopeless odds

At Albuoy's Point there is a small monument to the honour of His Majesty's Armed Cruiser *Jervis Bay*, which was sunk on Guy Fawkes night 1940. The brass plaque on the monument asks us to "Remember Captain E.S.F. Fegen, VC Royal Navy, the Officers and ship's company of HMS *Jervis Bay* who cheerfully gave their lives in successful defence of their convoy, fighting their ship to the last against hopeless odds Nov 5th 1940. Be Thou Faithfull unto Death." Tomorrow, a ceremony will take place at the monument as a part of Remembrance Day commemorations that honour the fallen dead of the two great wars of the last century, including 126 Bermudians.

The SS *Jervis Bay* began life in 1922 out of the great Vickers shipyards at Barrow in Furness in Northwestern England and was taken into the service of the Aberdeen & Commonwealth Line, which operated ships to and from Australia. All of their vessels were named for Australian bays, Jervis Bay being some 90 miles north of Sydney. After the outbreak of war between England and Germany in 1939, the ship was commandeered by the Royal Navy and fitted out with eight 6-inch guns. First sent on station to the South Atlantic, the vessel was assigned to Bermuda Convoy Escort Duty in May 1940, and from June 1940 to the Bermuda and Halifax Escort Service, a service that would last but a mere six months, ending its demise on November 5 at position 52.26N, 32.34W.

In its last days, *Jervis Bay* was the only armed escort for the 37 merchant ships of Convoy HX84, out of Halifax, Nova Scotia, bound for Great Britain. Meanwhile, the pocket battleship, KMS *Admiral Scheer* had broken out of the North Sea, making its way through the Denmark Strait between Greenland and Iceland en route to raid Allied shipping in the Atlantic Ocean. Convoy HX 84 became its prey in the dusk of November 5, 1940, as the sun set on the cold, grey reaches of the North Atlantic.

Captain Edward S. Fogarty Fegen, commanding officer of the *Jervis Bay,* immediately ordered the helmsman to set a beeline directly into the guns of the *Admiral Scheer*, to allow the convoy to scatter and escape as best it could. The *Jervis Bay* was out of action

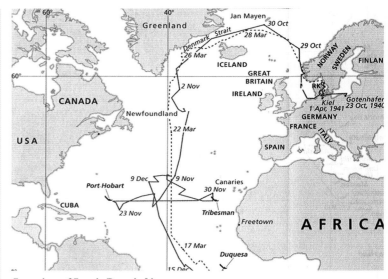

Location of Jervis Bay sinking

in 15 minutes and sank two hours later with the loss of 190 men, still drawing fire from the *Admiral Scheer*. Sixty-five of the crew were rescued by the Swedish vessel *Stureholm*. Captain Fegen was posthumously awarded the Victoria Cross, later donated to the Royal Naval Museum at Portsmouth by his daughter, Barbara Fegen. The citation for his VC notes his "Valour in challenging hopeless odds and giving his live to save the many ships it was his duty to protect."

The *Admiral Scheer* then proceeded to sink six other ships of the convoy, being the *Mopan, Maidan, Trewellard, Kenbane Head, Beaverford* and the *Fresno City*. A tanker, the *San Demetrio,* was also shelled and set afire, its crew abandoning ship. The ship was found by some of her crew in a lifeboat two days later, still on fire. They climbed back on board, put out the fires, repaired the engines and limped into port almost two weeks after the tanker was declared to be a loss, such is the courage of the merchant mariner.

In this David-and-Goliath battle, David lost unequivocally, as the odds were irrevocably stacked. The *Jervis Bay* had seven 6-inch Mark

Passenger ship **Jervis Bay** *in the late 1920s*

VII guns, examples of which can been seen at St. David's Battery, being manned in 1940 by the Bermuda Militia Artillery. The ship also had two 3-inch anti-aircraft guns, which figured little in the ensuing battle. It was the proverbial sitting duck, with guns half the range of its opponent.

The *Admiral Scheer* was sister ship to the Deutschland class *Lützow* and the *Admiral Graf Spee* of River Plate fame. She was refitted as a heavy cruiser and began raiding in November 1940, sinking 17 merchant ships for 114,000 gross tons. After "faultily concentrating her effort on the armed merchant cruiser *Jervis Bay*," she allowed Convoy HX84 to scatter. Thereafter the *Admiral Scheer* disrupted Allied shipping as far away as the Indian Ocean, returning to port in April 1941, having never been located by Allied hunter forces. Under Captain Theodor Krancke, the ship was the most successful capital commerce raider of the war. She was then used ineffectively in the Artic and Baltic and was sunk by RAF bombers in Kiel on April 9, 1945, later buried under a new dock. The colourised picture of the Admiral Scheer in 1937 was kindly supplied and copyright of Steve Wiper, *Classic Warships*, courtesy of John Asmussen, webmaster of www.deutschland-class.dk.

The raider weighed in at 16,200 gross tons, which could be propelled at almost 30 knots. It was commissioned in November 1934 with a length of 610 feet and a beam of 71 feet. The vessel mounted six 11-inch guns in two turrets of three; eight 5.9-inch guns and eight 21-inch torpedo tubes in two quadruple sets. The *Jervis Bay* never stood a chance with guns half the range of those on the state-of-the-art *Admiral Scheer*. Captain Fegan and his crew knowingly steered into the fires of hell, into order to allow the convoy to scatter by their sacrificial distraction: for this they must have our remembrance.

Si monumentum requiris, circumspice is the famous dictum referring to the many works in London of the great architect, Sir Christopher Wren. "If you wish to see his monuments, look around you," is what his son is supposed to have said. Look around you today and you will see the monuments to the fallen of the *Jervis Bay*, the 126 Bermudians and countless others who died in the line of duty in 1914–18 and 1939–45. Your prosperity owes much to those who sacrificed their all in those epic conflicts. Your freedoms of today are owed in great measure to those who accepted death for your lives of a free tomorrow. Remembrance Day, November 11, is a day for all to reflect, to remember with thanks the fallen, just as you would wish to be remembered had you ended your earthly term in the freezing oil-soaked waters of the North Atlantic all those years ago.

Admiral Scheer *transiting the Kiel Canal*

Commemorating boats from the sky

The year 1995 was a watershed year for Bermuda, as the Royal Navy left Bermuda after 200 years and the United States Navy steamed away after 54 years at two bases on the island. The eastern one, Kindley Field, named for First World War flying ace, Capt. Field Kindley, became Bermuda International Airport. The western Naval Operating Base was locked shut, though not for long due to the wiles of vandals and souvenir seekers.

From the early 1940s until the mid-1960s, the NOB was home to squadrons of flying boats, distinguished from seaplanes in having the lower part of their housing designed as a hull. As children camping on Hawkin's Island, we watched with wonder as these great bird-boats took off and landed in the ship's channel towards the Dockyard: it was our first contact with flying and the occasional navy blimp added to the mystery of the skies.

It was a flying boat from NOB that sank the third submarine claimed by the Americans after their entry into the war. On June 30, 1942, a Martin PBM Mariner of squadron VP-74, skippered by Lt. Richard E. Schreder, was returning to NOB after patrolling in the "Bermuda circle," when it found U-158 running fast on the surface.

Two P5M-2s fly over Gibbs Hill Lighthouse in the 1960s

After spotting the flying boat, the submarine dived, but a depth charge from the plane was lodged in its superstructure and detonated at its fused depth of 50 feet. The crew in the flying boat observed the underwater explosion of the submarine, which was lost with all hands.

After the war, flying boats continued to patrol out of Bermuda, using various planes, the last of which was the Martin P5M Marlin. The Glenn Martin Company in Maryland manufactured these extraordinary machines, which had an outstanding safety record. Martin, an aviation genius, made over 12,000 planes of 80 types over 40 years into the 1950s and his name survives as the familiar Lockheed Martin military corporation. He trained Boeing, Douglas, Lockheed and others who are household names today. Only one sample of the PBM Mariner and the P5M Marlin survive today, despite the large numbers made and their outstanding service records in the Second World War, Korea and Vietnam. These "fighting flying boats" were replaced by the PC-3 Orion airplanes, so familiar at Kindley Field to those of us who grew to maturity in Bermuda in the Cold War years, when they tracked Russian submarines en route to Cuba.

The 54 years of service of the US Navy at Bermuda was not without losses and one of those was the crash on September 22, 1961 of a P5M-2 of squadron VP-45. The flying boat was returning to Bermuda, when a fire destroyed one of its engines and it was forced to crash land in the ocean, 180 miles north of the island. Unfortunately, it hit the water at an angle and went straight down, with only three of the crew escaping from a depth of about 40 feet. The survivors, Jack Dockery, Peter Hofstedt and Patrick Imhof, remained together in rough seas for over 12 hours, until rescued around 8 a.m. the next day by the *African Pilot* of the Farrell Lines, out of New York for Monrovia.

One of the survivors, Patrick Imhof, AMS2, USN, was attacked by sharks during the rescue operation, but was plucked from the sea at the last moment. A memorial service was held at the Chapel of Peace at the naval station and base personnel erected a plaque in memory of their lost shipmates. When the station was closed in 1995, one of the items that went missing was that plaque.

Captain Andrew M. Sinclair, USN (Ret) and Lieutenant James Humphreys, USNR, have searched for the plaque for some years, but to no avail. They then decided to have a new one made and installed in the United States Navy Room at the Commissioner's House of the Bermuda Maritime Museum. Ken Henneberger, a member of VP-45 at the time, remained in Bermuda and will be assisting with a small exhibition on the Patrol Squadron and on the crash of 1961.

The United States Navy Room at the Commissioner's House commemorates the 54 years of service of the US Navy at Bermuda from 1941 to 1995, a period that saw the transformation of the island from a major military outpost to a tourism and international finance landmark. The US Navy Room was the gift of "plank owner" donors with American connections, including those named above, who have now donated the new plaque to remind us of those flying boat airmen who lost their lives at Bermuda in the service of the free world.

Capt. Andrew M. Sinclair, USN (Ret) and Lt. James Humphreys, USNR presenting the new plaque for VP-45 at Commissioner's House

Pomeroy: Flying Boats of Bermuda

Heavenly sentiments and earthly heritage

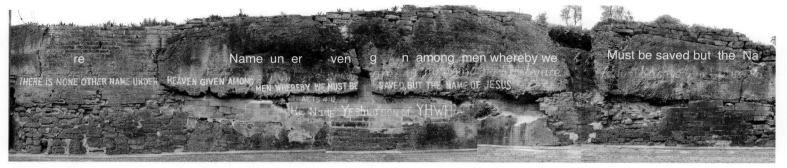

A composite photograph of the three religious inscriptions at the top of Scaur Hill, with overprinting to show what remains of the first one

Once across the smallest and now unusable drawbridge in the world, you enter God's Country, as some describe the island of Somerset. As if in reinforcement of that notion, as the land rises from The Scaur to the eminence that is straddled by a fort of the 1870s, the earthly voyager is greeted by religious graffiti writ large in white letters on the cliff face. The scene recently attracted much chatter on a local talk show, with many theories put forward about its origins. Despite its heavenly sentiments, no-one suggested that ET or friends had created the original inscription and most regarded it as part of Bermuda's earthly heritage.

In 1994, the second inscription was repainted, possibly in contravention to Caesar's law against graffiti in public places. That act inspired a copycat, who scrawled a new slogan below it, probably in breach of the law. Unknown to most, this last was the third piece of graffiti to have been painted at Scaur Hill and most speak of the second as if it were the first. Few are clear as to the date and creator of the first or the second writings, but the third is dated to 2004, inscriber unknown.

The archaeology of the scene shows that the first inscription extended further to the north than the second. It is mostly faded away and was truncated by a driveway through the cliff. The first and second writings are from the Bible, King James Version. They state: "There is none other name under Heaven given among men, whereby we must be saved, but the Name of Jesus." The first part is an excerpt from Acts 4.12, with "but the Name of Jesus" added on. As can be seen from the photograph on which I have overprinted the surviving letters of the first inscription, the "me" of Name and the words "of Jesus" have been destroyed by the driveway.

That destruction may be the reason why the inscription was repainted further towards Somerset Bridge at some unknown date. The original was written in italics, while the second is in a Roman typeface. The 2004 addition reads: "He Name Yeshua son of YHWH." The last letters stand for Yahweh or God the Father. A religious person writes: "Thus we are justified in saying that YAHWEH and YAHSHUA (Jesus) are, to all intents and purposes, indistinguishable as far as their common Name is concerned. Yahweh is the Father—and Yahweh is the Son." The Scaur Hill writings reflect a controversy of religious thought, as some claim Yahshua is the true name of Jesus and thus Jesus should not be used.

Those religious comments aside, we return to the earthly question of who painted the first edition of the Scaur Hill inscriptions. The Bermuda National Trust's outstanding book on the architecture of Sandys Parish says that the father of Samuel George Brown (who until 1932 owned the home near The Scaur now called "Watch House") painted the slogan in gratitude for a good harvest. James, the father, lived at Church Hill further north in Somerset and died in 1906, aged about 77. So if James was the first graffiti artist at Scaur Hill, the original painting must have been executed before 1906.

This would fit with part of it being destroyed by the driveway probably cut out in the 1930s. Another factor that may help to date the work was the construction of Scaur Hill Fort in the 1870s, as it may be likely the present level of the road at the top of the hill was created by the military. It is possible that the original road passed over the hill at a higher grade, which was reduced into the present cutting to accommodate the ditch of the fort, which crossed the road just north of the position of the inscriptions. A long-lost wooden bridge would have allowed passage for the road over the ditch. If the military created the cutting and cliff face, the first painting would have to have been made after the mid-1870s and before 1906.

The second inscription is therefore possibly dated after the 1930s, depending on the construction of the house roadway that cut through part of the original. It is the second version that has become part of local lore and heritage, but it likely came after the death of Farmer Brown by several decades. While not the original, it is of significant antiquity to stand in for James Brown's original artistry. It can thus be "grandfathered" as earthly heritage, beyond the reach of the modern laws against graffiti, though not necessarily protected by legislation for antiquities.

The same cannot be said of the third inscription, which is no different than the civilian graffiti that is unfortunately sprouting up all over the island. Such graffiti detracts from the beauty of Bermuda and degrades its heritage and tourism assets. The Bible says: "Render therefore unto Caesar the things which are Caesar's; and unto God the things that are God's" (Matthew 22:21). Caesar would probably prefer that his earthly walls be not rendered with thoughts more appropriate for private heavenly communication.

Islands lost in the northern Atlantic

The Free French submarine Surcouf

"*Recent events have put in the limelight the Islands of Bermuda, situated a thousand kilometers off the coast of the eastern U.S., at latitude similar to Charleston and Casablanca and that feature an array of interesting geographical characteristics. Those isles are in fact a coral atoll…lost in the northern Atlantic. Our illustrious colleague the Admiral A. Lepotier, who knows very well those British islands, explains in this article their peculiar geological formation as well as their interesting strategic (and tourist!) features.*"

Thus the editor of the French magazine *Géographia* in July 1953 opens an article on the new world order at Bermuda. In the essay, retired Rear Admiral Lepotier, a visitor to Bermuda in 1943, gave his views on "this tropical paradise that got lost north of the Tropic of Cancer." Due to its geological structure and geographical position, the island was becoming "in the current state of world political and economic affairs an important strategic base and also the 'Riviera' for New Yorkers." The Admiral thus identified the coming twin pillars of the Bermuda economy, military expenditures and tourist spending, mostly from the U.S. Modern events and Samsons of sorts have largely brought down these pillars and it remains to be seen if the temple of Bermuda can be held up and restored by newer types of financial underpinnings.

Adolphe-Auguste Lepotier was born in Nantes in 1898. A sailor during the First World War, he entered the French school for naval officers in 1919, eventually serving at sea in the Second World War. He was at the pivotal and controversial battle of Mers El Kebir on July 3, 1940, when the British sank several French warships to prevent their possession by the Germans, who had recently occupied France. In 1944, he took part in the relief of Corsica, after a visit to the western Atlantic and Bermuda in 1943. Lepotier was appointed rear admiral in 1952 and retired two years later to devote his life to research and writing of naval history. He died in his eightieth year in 1978.

Via the BBC, Charles de Gaulle in his famous "Appeal of June the 18th" speech asked his countrymen to continue to fight against Germany, but four days later on June 22, 1940, Pétain signed the surrender. Parts of the French military were out of the country and ultimately joined de Gaulle and his Forces Françaises Libres, or the "Free French" *en anglais*.

Bermuda was familiar with the Free French navy, which had some 50 ships and almost 4,000 men serving with the Royal Navy. The most famous of the fleet to visit the island was the mega-submarine *Surcouf*, which had its own ensign with the initials "CG," in honour of the Free French leader. Surrounded by controversy from its capture by the British on July 3, 1940, *Surcouf* was sent to Bermuda in June 1941, but from late July to late November, the boat was refitted in New England. On February 12, 1942, the submarine left Bermuda for the Pacific theatre, via the Panama Canal but was never seen again. There are various legends surrounding her end, but "disregarding the

Destroyers Simoun *(left) and* Tempete, *which visited Bermuda in 1943. At right, ensigns of the Free French Navy (top) and of the* Surcouf

EDWARD HARRIS

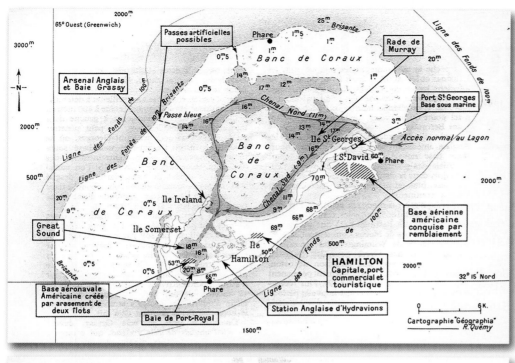

GÉOGRAPHIA

REVUE D'INFORMATIONS ET D'ACTUALITÉS GÉOGRAPHIQUES

N° 22 JUILLET 1953 150 FR.

Cover of 1953 Géographia

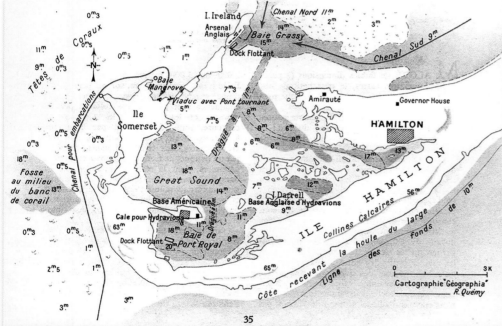

Lepotier's charts of Bermuda

largest "river" in the world. "That trans-Atlantic 'central heating system' starts straight out of the Florida Channel, then curves eastward as if to serve Bermuda as its first and favourite client, snubbing the American coastline which is subject to the icy Labrador Current." He mentions the importation of African slaves, who acquired "excellent reputations as able seamen and fishermen, helping in the design of a special type of rig called Bermuda sails."

He then discusses the building of the American bases, as "I was stationed on the island in the spring of 1943 while the group of escort ships I was in command of was renovated at the Ireland Island Arsenal and Base. I witnessed then those rapid developments and transformations of the local geography that were necessitated by strategic considerations" of the war. After reviewing its charms for tourists, Lepotier concludes: this "oasis" that some caprice of geography positioned amid abyssal depths in this predestined point hides beneath its poetic charm some hydrographic realities that make it one of the major strategic bases of the modern world.

To underscore the hydrographic realities, Lepotier's charts (reproduced here) are the work of a seaman, if one knew not the author. They emphasise the channels and anchorages of vital naval importance, the lands of Bermuda almost a faded backdrop: "the 'Honeymoon Islands' are beaded around those 'strategic points.'" Writing today, he would have to say that the honeymoon is over on both counts and that the only channels worth navigating are between the banks of Front Street and the ends of the rainbow on Pitts Bay Road.

Postscript: The author thanks Bermuda resident Eugene Durenard for his translation of Admiral Lepotier's article. His father, oceanographer Dr. Alexis Durenard of France has given a copy of the *Géographia* magazine to the Bermuda Maritime Museum.

predictable [one] about her being swallowed by the Bermuda Triangle," it is likely *Surcouf* was accidentally sunk by collision with the American freighter, *Thompson Lykes*, this side of the Panama Canal on February 18, 1942. Lost with all hands, it was the world's greatest submarine disaster to that date.

The following year, Captain Lepotier arrived at Bermuda in command of a warship flotilla of the Free French Navy, for refitting and supply. He was captain of the *Tempete* ("Tempest," appropriately for the island, and for Lepotier, built at Nantes his birthplace), in the company of the *Simoun*, both Bourrasque Class destroyers. Other ships in the group included Elan Class minesweepers *Gazelle*, *Commandant Bory* and *Commandant Delage*. The officers and crew had a very pleasant stay on the island, as attested by letters of thanks written to the Bermuda Ladies League, according to information on Keith Forbes' website, Bermuda-online.org.

Lepotier's article reminds us of the unique position of Bermuda as the northernmost coral atoll, bathed by the warm Gulf Stream, the

Rare guns should be big draw for tourism

One day in 1929, a young American was sent to the island for a period of rest and he spent much of his time exploring the forts. A second visit several years later ignited a lifelong interest in Bermuda's fortifications and in 1962, Colonel Roger Willock, USMC, privately published *Bulwark of Empire*, his seminal work on those historic structures. In 1984, the Bermuda Maritime Museum republished his book and the Colonel came for its presentation. With this doyen of Bermuda forts, we visited Fort Cunningham on Paget Island, the most important fort in the island of the 1870s.

As the last Bermuda-built brig, *Cedrine*, was headed for disaster on its maiden voyage on the shores of the Isle of Wight in 1862, the sea-world of canvas and wooden ships was irrevocably changing. The British, in response to French shipbuilding initiatives, had just launched *Warrior*, the world's first iron ship. This outstanding invention, today restored at Portsmouth, England, marked the start of the modern arms race—a race no-one is likely to win, but one that will probably be with us until the end of mankind. A vessel of hybrid power of sail and steam, the *Warrior* is connected to Bermuda, for in 1869, along with the *Black Prince* and the *Terrible*, she towed the industrial wonder of the day, the great floating dock, HMS *Bermuda*, to the island via the Azores. The bones of the pontoons and the hull of the floating dock are yet sunk and rotting at Spanish Point and were an intimate and mysterious part of many local childhoods.

The iron ships were built as a necessary response to the invention in the later 1850s of a new type of cannon, the breech, or rear, loading rifled gun that fired an elongated projectile, rather than the cannonball of old. With a projectile, the weight of the bullet can be increased several times over that of a round cannonball for the same diameter, or caliber, of the bore of the gun barrel. Projectiles could pierce through the wooden walls of a sailing ship with ease and in a gunshot, the navies of the world became obsolete.

The stone of Bermuda's forts was akin to the timber of the floating fortresses of those navies and was no match for the projectiles of rifled guns. In Bermuda and throughout the world, the designers of forts reacted to the advent of the iron ship and projectile weapons with new engineering creations. None was more exotic than Bermuda's Fort Cunningham, of which one parliamentarian at Westminster rhetorically asked: "Is it made of gold, as it has cost so much to build?"

Fort Cunningham began its life as one of the six great works erected in St. George's Parish in the 1820s to protect the Narrows Channel, the key to Bermuda's inner harbours and the Dockyard to the west. It was built of the hard Bermuda limestone, quarried at the Dockyard or at Ferry Reach, and was set in a polygonal ditch with reverse fires, the coming fashion in fortifications. It was armed with smooth bore guns firing cannon balls and had a new type of draw-bridge at the entrance over the ditch, parts of which survive.

Volunteers from EARTHWATCH excavate the RMLs in 1991.
Left: Fort Cunningham

In response to the iron-ship and projectile-gun revolution of the 1850s, the gun level of Fort Cunningham was rebuilt to contain two massive walls of wrought-iron plates. One was for two guns and the other was for five huge Rifled Muzzle Loaders. The life of those weapons was short-lived and in 1882 the invention of gun steel ensured their rapid obsolescence. Fort Cunningham was again rebuilt in the 1890s for two of the new steel breech loading rifles and the existing 166 tons of wrought iron RMLs in its casemates presented a major disposal problem.

Colonel Willock was always of the opinion that the RMLs were simply buried at the fort. So it proved in January 1991, when the Bermuda Maritime Museum and an EARTHWATCH team under the leadership of Professor Richard Gould of Brown University, conducted an archaeological excavation at Fort Cunningham under the auspices of the National Parks Commission and the Bermuda Parks Department.

Seven great RMLs were discovered thrown into the ditch and were seen, much to his delight and prediction, by Colonel Willock on his last visit to Bermuda in 1992. Five of the guns are a mere 18 tons apiece and two weigh in at 38 tons each. The latter are the biggest RMLs, outweighed only by the two 100-ton guns at Gibraltar and Malta, and only some eight survive worldwide. The smallest RMLs weigh only half a ton and Bermuda has several. In all we have 40 of this type of revolutionary gun. This collection, along with the iron fronted Fort Cunningham, is without parallel in the world of historic artillery and could be the big bangers of Bermuda's cultural tourism.

EDWARD HARRIS

Limestone: bedrock of Bermuda culture

Bermuda is a house of sand. Standing some 16,000 feet, or three miles, off the seabed in the area of the North Atlantic known as the Bermuda Rise, the island is nothing more than a large sand dune perched on the summit of a long-extinct oceanic volcano. So while we continue to build up our sandcastle of 393 years—independent or otherwise—some reflection on our origin and its connection to Bermuda's outstanding heritage in stone might be in order.

The formation of Bermuda began over 100 million years ago, when a hot spot in the mantle of the Earth began to erupt under the sea. Slowly and solidly, the basalts and other volcanic rocks built up a mountain that one day broke through the surface. Like Hawaii or Montserrat, it became one of nature's great fireworks displays, probably ending the light show some 5,000 feet above the sea. That is a far cry from the present highest point on the island at Town Hill, Smith's Parish, which at 258 feet is some 200 feet shorter that Khufu's Great Pyramid at Giza.

The sea eroded the volcano, the waves working a destructive wonder until Mount Bermuda sank below the swells, leaving a shelf some 32 miles in diameter, with two smaller plateaus at Argus and Challenger Banks. Coral began to grow on the undersea mountaintop and the world's northernmost atoll took shape. Then about a million years ago, the Ice Ages came into being, locking up much of the water on the planet and sea levels dropped up to 600 feet. The atoll was exposed and its reefs ground into sand by the sea. Winds drove the sand into dunes and Bermuda as we know it was founded.

Some of the dunes were eventually turned into rock by the corrosive action of rain, which combines with carbon dioxide in the air to make

The Coney Island military lime kiln from the air in the 1980s

a weak carbonic acid. Since the sand is derived from seashells, it is a type of calcium carbonate and is dissolved by the acid. The liquid thus produced solidifies upon drying and Bermuda limestone is created. The older the stone formation, the harder it becomes, as more liquid seeps into its pores. Thus, one day we will have to paint the limestone of the Dockyard ramparts, as the same geological forces that made the stone is dissolving it today. This process can be seen at the entrance of the Bermuda Maritime Museum, where the liquid is making stalactites on the ceiling of the gateway, stalagmites on the road and flowstone down the wall surfaces.

The making of lime for cement and the working of limestone for building is a tradition several thousand years old and the first settlers in the early 1600s would have been aware of such methods. The essential building ingredient was lime, which was produced by burning stone that had a high content of calcium carbonate. For this the older and very hard Bermuda limestone, such as found at Dockyard, was needed. The lime rock was layered with wood in a lime kiln, which burnt for some days, the stone reducing to powder or lime. The last burning of a kiln was in 1990 at Ferry Reach by the late Orville Bascome of St. George's.

Nearby on Coney Island is the finest lime kiln in Bermuda, which was built by the Royal Engineers in the mid-1800s. Recently my friend and lime expert, Ken Uracius, looked at this monument to industry and tradition and declared: "It's a continuous burn." Unlike the civilian kilns, this one was designed to burn rock around the clock and was lined with brick to cope with the intense heat generated by the process.

Another military kiln exists at Ferry Reach Park, somewhat infested with Mexican peppers; and Paul and Penne Leseur rediscovered a civilian kiln at Hog Bay Park after Hurricane Fabian swept away vegetation. In Britain, the process of making lime was industrialised and most of the individual kilns have been lost. The Bermudian kilns are small monuments to an ancient building method and an essential part of the traditions of the island that produced our outstanding domestic architecture.

Being of the same material, the mortars of lime mixed with local sand were completely sympathetic to Bermuda stone. The lime also provided the paint for Bermuda roofs and many of us remember the barrel of lime and water in the back yard, awaiting a little stirring and the application of paintbrushes. Modern Portland cement is not sympathetic to Bermuda stone, for it is too hard and does not breathe. The restoration of old Bermuda buildings should be undertaken with lime mortars, sadly not now generally used.

Lest we completely forget what our forebears and some still alive remember, Ken and I have it in mind to restore the kiln at Coney Island and have a continuous burn once again, transforming rock around the clock. The lime produced could be used in the restoration of the fortifications for which it was built in the first place.

The late Orville Bascome with the last burn of his Ferry Reach kiln in 1990

Foreign bones at Mullet Bay

The schooner **Priscilla** *lies at anchor in Mullet Bay. Below: Captain John Frederick Leseur, who navigated* **Priscilla** *to Turks & Caicos in 1907*

Death is the great leveller and it is possible that bones become Bermudian once they are buried; perhaps some authority can give us an opinion. In the meantime, there are a lot of foreign bones in Bermuda, human and otherwise. My dear friends from England, Rohan and Margaret Sturdy, saviours of the Commissioner's House, are interred at St. James' Church in Somerset. Discovered recently at that place of worship was the "Strangers' Crypt," reserved for those persons who passed Immigration and Customs unable to fill out the forms, being in the hands of their Maker. Having died at sea, if the religion of such strangers was not known they were not allowed to be buried in the consecrated churchyard, hence the reserved crypt for "religious expats"—in modern jargon.

The bones of present interest are metaphorical, being the remains of an American schooner, *Priscilla*, still visible through the murky waters of Mullet Bay in St. George's Parish. Whether the last owners, Messrs. Manson and Neun of Rochester, New York abandoned claim to her is not known, but it is unlikely that any would dispute that *Priscilla*'s bones are a part of Bermuda's underwater cultural heritage.

Next year [2006] is the 100th anniversary of the world's premier ocean race, now called the Newport-Bermuda Race. *Priscilla*, the schooner, first came to the island in the second race in 1907. *The Royal Gazette* reported that on June 5, 1907, 13 yachts were making sail for the 10 a.m. start of the Race from the Brooklyn Yacht Club, competing for the Maier Cup, given by Frank of that name, Commodore of the New Rochelle Yacht Club. At 80 feet, *Priscilla* was one of the largest boats in the race and sailed under the flag of the Rochester Yacht Club.

In this way *Priscilla* came to be in Bermuda, where a few weeks later it was decided to make a run to the Turks & Caicos for a cargo of salt. She had been purchased the previous year from the Gorton-Pew Fisheries Company of Gloucester, Massachusetts by Henry P. Neun of Rochester, having been built of wood at the former town in 1891, with a burden of 53 tons, a beam of 22 feet and drawing eight feet.

Mary Ellen Parry, the daughter of Henry Neun, gave details of the *Priscilla* to Paul Leseur some years ago. An account of the voyage to the Turks & Caicos in July 1907 was published later that year and John Leseur has given a surviving copy of the booklet to the Bermuda Maritime Museum. Details on the trip are taken from the booklet and in late June 1907 a cargo of lumber was boarded; whether of Bermuda cedar was not declared.

EDWARD HARRIS

Nothing changes, it seems, in bureaucracy and *the shipping of the crew was carried on with all the gravity and red tape that may have attended the shipping of six hundred men to a fifteen-thousand-ton frigate of forty guns.* Aside from Master H. Kruger, the compliment was recruited locally, with names many will recognise. The mate was J. C. Crisson; Seamen were R. Linley, A. Harriott and Charles Leseur. The cook was P. Anderson and the cabin boy J. Tucker.

The navigating officer was Captain John Frederick Leseur (in whose honour John and Betsy Leseur and Paul and Penne Leseur donated a room in the Commissioner's House). There were four others, F. Selley, W. Spencer. O. Petty and W. Wilson, to *each of whom a post of importance was assigned,* though not described. An old yellow cat appeared as a stowaway on deck as the *Priscilla* made for the Narrows and the open sea on July 2, 1907.

The southern run to Grand Turk took 10 days, the return to Bermuda only eight. Five days were spent in the islands, with salt being loaded at Cockburn Town in East Caicos. *The salt is filled into half-bushel bags and then carried by the boatmen, five to six bags at a load, upon their heads, to the lighters. Instances of these powerful men carrying as many as seven bags, a weight of over 300 lbs., are of common occurrence.*

From left: Archie "Pat" Burrows, Wilfred Arnold "Indian" Outerbridge Sr., Clyde Leseur and Captain Charles Stoneham of the tour boat Priscilla *in the 1950s*

Title page of Priscilla *booklet*

On board, the bags were emptied into the hold where trimmers with shovels leveled the salt for the voyage. In the Turks & Caicos, salt was made by evaporation of seawater in some 700 acres of *salinas* or salt ponds. Until nationalisation in the early 1950s, the Harriott Family of Bermuda and the Turks Islands made the last salt there on Salt Cay.

The *Priscilla* arrived back in Bermuda on July 24, 1907 and may have never gone to sea again. The boat sprang a leak at anchor in 1911, which proved fatal and sank near Banjo Island at Mullet Bay. Teredo worms, the flightless termites of the sea, did the rest. As with human remains only the bones, the strongest part of the body, survived in the form of the keel and ribs.

In the 1950s, Clyde Leseur, grandson of Captain John Frederick, son of Charles and father of John and Paul, bought a war surplus air-sea rescue boat from the U.S. Navy for use as a cruise ship in Bermuda. An awning and seating for tourists replaced the gun turret, the twin high-octane 1,400 h.p. engines were supplanted by conventional diesel motors, and the boat was renamed *Priscilla* in honour of the Leseurs of the schooner crew. The new *Priscilla* began daily tours to St. George's and ushered in a famous era of local cruise ships in the tourism trade. It continues to this day with operators such as Donald and Derek Morris' "Bermuda Island Cruises," though Clyde Leseur's *Priscilla* is itself as much a part of the bones of the past as its namesake in the muds of Mullet Bay.

Loading bagged salt onto a lighter

Salt Ponds at the Turks & Caicos

Barnes Corner: a fork in Bermuda's road?

For several years, I have conducted surveillance on two man-made rocks at Barnes Corner in the parish of Southampton. The corner is in reality a fork where the only road from Somerset divides into Middle and South Roads.

At this fork is situated a small triangle of grass, hemmed in by the hideous concrete curbstones that were once a decade ago very fashionable with the roadworks people in government. At that time, much of the South Road was plastered with these ugly curbs, removing the grass verge that made it possible for tourists to escape the predations of the ever present Bermuda tailgater.

At Barnes Corner, the little triangular oasis of grass is decorated with a lump of hard Bermuda limestone and a telephone pole. Then one day about three years ago, a construction truck added more decoration to this roadside tableau by dumping several concrete blocks off the side of the vehicle, hitting the limestone lump as opposed to passing tourist. Later on, in the wee hours of a weekend morning, a container with a built-in generator for a visiting submarine at Dockyard, fell onto the road and into the triangle in an unscheduled stop. The container ploughed into the asphalt of the road and into the soil of the triangle, throwing some of the soil against the limestone rock, mixing it in with the shattered concrete block. The soil was never cleared away.

Living in the Upper Parishes, I commute to Hamilton and beyond several times a week and take the fork in the road to travel the more scenic South Shore Road. So Barnes Corner and I have a long relationship and for three of those years, I have been watching to see how long the broken concrete blocks would remain so decorously draped over the limestone rock at this junction: they are still there.

Nearby, on the other side of the Middle Road where it joins the Railway Trail, there is the other rock I have been watching. It is a small concrete pillar that is a boundary stone marking the northern limit of the Railway right-of-way. It was placed there by the Public Works Department, probably in the late 1940s, when ownership of the Bermuda Railway passed to the government. Several more such markers can be prominently seen in front of the nearby Glasgow Lodge. These markers are special historic monuments and once existed in quantity throughout Bermuda, most notable on the original South Shore Road that was built from Tucker's Town to Warwick Camp and beyond by the British military. Some of these are in plain view near Spittal Pond, so much so that you could almost drive over them.

This appears to be what happened with the monument at Barnes Corner. One day it was proud and erect, the next it was tipped over at a severe angle. One suspects a hit-and-run event. A year ago, my brother was visiting home and I took him and a shovel to the spot of the crime. After much ado, we righted the boundary stone and went home satisfied with this public service. Lo and behold, a couple of

Broken concrete blocks atop the rock and triangle of grass at Barnes Corner. Inset, Andrew Harris with the displaced PWD boundary stone of the Bermuda Railway right-of-way

months later, the stone was again Bermuda's leaning Tower of Pisa and so it remains. Since no seismic activity has been recorded of late, cold case instincts lead one to believe that the stone has again been run over by a vehicle. The driver clearly could not be bothered to repair the damage so caused.

So endeth my scientific survey on the two rocks at Barnes Corner. It may be concluded that no officials are in charge of these public areas and monuments, for surely they would have noticed the junk concrete blocks and damaged boundary stone over the last three years and rectified both situations. Secondly, the members of the public who dumped the concrete blocks and twice tipped over the boundary marker apparently had no interest in cleaning up or repairing the damage they caused to the environment.

This process of trashing our own back yard is being repeated all over Bermuda. Do the examples from Barnes Corner reflect a mere turn in the road, or rather a major negative fork in our appreciation and care for the heritage paradise for which we are but temporary trustees?

Tourism: our most appropriate industry

In 1945, the War ended, but the conflict over Bermuda's built heritage was soon to begin. Starting in 1951 and ending in 1995, the Bermuda Government inherited the major lands, historic buildings and monuments of the military forces, residents of the island for over three centuries. The destruction of many of the historic buildings of these properties followed, not by enemy bombs but through the slow burn of our own hands, as committee after committee and government after government failed to appreciate the significance of this legacy and its place in Bermuda's only true industry, tourism.

Many of you are prone to say in these money-washed days from non-tourism sources that tourism is dead. If tourism is dead, so is the built heritage of this paradise, as there will be no reason to keep any of it, for there will be no visitors to view it. It remains the almost complete failure of those in the right places to appreciate the connection between tourism and the preservation and well being of Bermuda's built heritage, military and domestic. Tourism is rooted in the concept of touring to see unique monuments, outstanding landscapes and different peoples and their cultures. It was such an appropriate cultural environment that made Bermuda tourism great in earlier years.

An example of this failure is seen through a rare booklet entitled *Bermuda: Fact Manual for Industry*. In it industry means nuts and bolts, grease and mechanical hardware, not the software of the tourism trade that is the ambience we know and love as Bermuda itself, its landscape and built heritage. The purpose of the booklet, published by the Bermuda Crown Lands Corporation—the precursor to the just as inaptly named Bermuda Land Development Corporation —was to attract nuts and bolt industries to the island. This was as forlorn a hope in the 1950s as it is these 50 years later. Since the departure of the military in 1995, the only industrial magnets this island can attract are people (tourism) and finance (the so-called "international business"—but what business is more international than tourism?), neither of which is very greasy.

The guinea pigs for the Crown Lands industry initiative were the sites inherited from the British military from 1957, when the garrison finally departed Bermuda. The Dockyard, Prospect and St. George's Camps, their buildings and associated fortifications were the grist for this new government pepper mill. These were lands, like those later in Tucker's Town and St. David's Island that were appropriated from private owners—black, white and other—from 1809 onwards. Of course, the land was not returned to those original owners, but put in the local government pork barrel. Few overseas industries were attracted

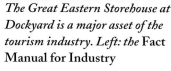

The Great Eastern Storehouse at Dockyard is a major asset of the tourism industry. Left: the **Fact Manual for Industry**

to these historic sites, but many weird local businesses flourished for a while on the cheap rents offered in the business parks of Dockyard and elsewhere. Any idea was given credence, but few "industries" long survived, despite the built-in benefits and lack of planning controls. Some of these businesses destroyed the buildings they used, either directly, or because they were demolished afterwards, for, in the usual words of the uncaring bureaucrat: "They had become unhealthy and unsafe."

The *Fact Manual for Industry* relates mainly to the Dockyard and has some interesting statistics. We are informed that "the supply of labour is adequate and intelligent" and that "full governmental cooperation is assured." The local population stood at 42,640 souls, 10,686 Armed Forces and 2,730 "Transients." By 1964, annual visitors had reached 203,434, a figure tourism doomsayers think we are reaching today, but by decline, not increase. We are told the largest export was to the U.K., for a princely sum of £223,737 and the smallest was a pauper's purse to Denmark for £2,310. In total, exports were less than three-quarters of a million pounds, against imports of over nine million pounds from the US alone!

The industry initiative of the 1950s and 1960s, while well meaning, must be considered an abject failure for business, and for the built heritage it exploited, it was a disaster. At the Dockyard lands, over 50 buildings were ultimately destroyed, many of outstanding historical value. Since then at Dockyard, the only appropriate "industry" has proved to be that of tourism.

A hand and glove relationship exists between tourism and the preservation of the built environment. Tourism ensures the preservation of heritage and that heritage ensures the delight and abiding interest of the visitor. The nuts and bolts of the financial "international business" is money: their business is to preserve capital, not heritage.

The fact is that tourism is Bermuda's most appropriate industry. Heritage is its raw material and finished product; fortunately we have some left. The fact is that sound tourism depends on the preservation of the historic environment—which created and sustains the tourist-loved ambience called Bermuda. The fact is that we are constantly told that tourism is dead. The fact is that that self-fulfilling prophecy is the seed of our downfall as a people and the ruination of the outstanding built heritage of Bermuda.

News from the Front, Christmas, 1915

An envelope from Bermuda to Harold Trimingham. At right, the Bermuda Machine Gunners' Christmas card from France

Editor's note: This unsent letter was recently found in a private archive by Dr. Harris, who thought it should be published at this time of year [December 23, 2005], with illustrations from the Godet and Trimingham Collections at the Bermuda Maritime Museum.

"This is a letter to my great-grandchildren now that Christmas, a time for thanksgiving and remembrance, is upon us once again. When I was young, we were embroiled in the Great War and I did a small part, especially at Christmas, to send parcels of goods and clothing to our Bermudian boys serving in the muddy trenches of France.

This was a war that went through four Christmases and consumed the lives of 80 Bermudians, as well as millions of others. Your lives of plenty today are founded, as are those of all Bermudians, on the blood of our men lost in the Great War and the one that followed less than a generation later. Some of our young lads went over in the first Spring of the war, nine months after the "Guns of August" uttered their salvos to create the first "no man's land" of the vast

Postcard of the Allied Countries 1914–18

killing fields of Europe. The First Contingent of the Bermuda Volunteer Rifle Corps went straight into the trenches in June 1915 and by Christmas five were already dead. Our family supported Private C. A. Adams and he wrote to me on the first Christmas in the trenches with news from the Front. I have asked that my grandchildren, your parents, keep this and other letters so that the bravery of our Bermudian soldiers and the horrors they went through are not forgotten, but thought you might like to read it at this holiday season.

Dear Friend: A few lines thanking you for the Card which I got in the trenches last night and was pleased to get. Well Xmas will be here & gone by the time you get this so I must wish you & Mr. Godet & Thomas a Happy New Year. I think we shall spend Christmas in the trenches so will write and tell you all about it later on.

The stove you sent me [has] come in very good for last night we had a nasty frost & about two o'clock in the morning I took it out of my pocket & got some water & oxos & made me a good drink so I must thank you again for the stove.

The trenches we are now in are rotten. We are up to our knees in water & mud and it is so cold that all the woollen goods you made for me before I left Bda are a godsend or else I should be freezing. Please give my best wishes to Mr. Godet & Thomas and tell them that I hope it is warmer there [than] here. We are now expecting to get a few days leave very shortly & I think we all need it for we have been out here now over six months & it is over eight months since we sailed from Bermuda.

There is one thing I can say & that is that I do not regret being with the Boys for we are all just like brothers & when we lose one we are all heartbroken. We have lost five of our boys now but they died for the Country & I know that they will never be forgotten by the people of Bermuda, who are praying day by day for us & I am sure that the Lord is answering their prayers.

Well dear friend we are all looking forward to going out of the trenches to see what parcels there are for us for we cannot get them in the trenches for it is too wet & muddy so we have to wait until our time is up for being relieved. I have not received any socks from Mrs. Tucker yet but hope to later on for we have to change them now twice a day if possible so as to keep our feet warm.

No one can realise what we are going through unless they come and see for themselves for I would not like to try & tell you some of our hardships out here. But for all of them I don't mind as long as I am doing my duty & trying to make a name from Bermuda.

Well I must now close as I am so cold. Hoping to hear from you soon. Believe me to be yours truly. Pte C. A. Adams. Wishing you a happy New Year from the trenches.

Private Adams was one of the 125 riflemen of the BVRC and 234 gunners of the Bermuda Militia Artillery who served in Europe. All of these men spent several Christmases away from home in the worst war the world has ever witnessed. Adams survived three long years and Christmases in the trenches: he is a changed man.

Many families suffered great losses; in the case of the Triminghams, two of four brothers were killed. Joseph Trimingham would probably be pleased that his grave in France is red soil covered by nasturtiums, which bloom in the red earth here at Christmas. Your great uncle, Lennock de Graaf Godet, was one of Bermuda's first airmen and he was lost over France in 1918. The graves of some of our men overseas have never been visited. I did hear of late that some of Stanley Parker Wadson's family were finally able to see his grave and it was a very emotional and evocative occasion for his son and granddaughter.

One day, children, you will inherit some of the material things that Mr. Godet and I had the use of in our lives. You have already inherited a life of unparalleled prosperity, which could have been otherwise had the war gone down in defeat. You have also inherited a spiritual debt to all the Bermudians who are in final rest in foreign fields. I hope that this Christmas and those to come that you will take a moment from your festivities to remember and give thanks to those who gave the gift of their lives for all your tomorrows."

—*Mrs. J. D. Middleton Godet*

Postscript: Priscilla Matilda Godet, wife of J.D.M. Godet and mother of Thomas M. du B. Godet, died in Bermuda in 1952. She had two grandchildren: Tom Godet, who died 2002 and Molly Godet Thomas of Bermuda. Molly has given the Godet family papers pertaining to the First World War to the Bermuda Maritime Museum for its military archives.

Above and below: Charles Gray Gosling Gilbert in the trenches

Grave of Joseph Trimingham in France, photographed in 1923

Commissioner's House: Bermuda's stone frigate

In the early 1980s, the late Fred Lumsden and I would wander through the ruin that was the Commissioner's House at the Maritime Museum ruminating on the past, as is the wont of antiquarians. Fred would often end his recollections—for he worked in the House in its last operational days during the Second World War—with "We went ashore to the Dockyard canteen," or such like. It was some time before I appreciated that his turn of phase, or tack, was due to the fact that the Commissioner's House from 1919 to 1951 was a ship—Bermuda's first stone frigate, HMS Malabar—the sixth of seven to bear that name in the annals of the Royal Navy. It is a pity that in those days, the museum did not have its oral history department in being, for we could have recorded Fred's interesting recollections on DVD for future generations.

Be that as it was, Fred was living the life of Royal Navy personnel, all of whom were obliged to serve on board a ship. So naval stations were given the name of one of

HMS Malabar VI (1919–1951), aka Commissioner's House, restored to its original glory, complete with bow-chaser

HMS Malabar V (1866–1919), aka HMS Terror, with the Star of India emblazoned on the bow

His or Her Majesty's Ships and if the vessel was scrapped or sold on, the name was transferred to a building. The last HMS Malabar (VII) was the headquarters building of the Royal Navy at Bermuda, Moresby House. It yet stands on the left, somewhat damaged by the recent hurricane, just over Cockburn Cut Bridge, the first such crossing apparently in Bermuda to have been made of concrete.

The first four *Malabars* were wooden warships of a type that ruled the ocean seas for nigh on 300 years, until the British launched the *Warrior* in 1862, the first iron battleship. The *Malabar* for which the ships were named is a beautiful section of the western coast of India. The first *Malabars* were used to protect the sea routes and trade to that sub-continent.

British troops were transported where "the sun never sets," in peace and war, on ships. My Bermudian grandmother, Agnes Matilda Whitecross, once travelled that way, being on station with her husband, William Sidney Harris, Royal Fusiliers, at Mauritius and India in the years before the First World War. All of their children were thus born in far-flung places, with the exception of the last being delivered here.

My grandfather killed himself here in Bermuda, a victim, my father always said, of the First World War, as he carried a steel plate in his skull to cover injuries that left him in a vulnerable mental state. Granny was left to bring up a battery of children and a grandson, but died at the venerable age of 96.

The British Army is seen as a "projectile fired by the British fleet," for excepting two land battles on the home front, the force has had to be transported by sea to all its other engagements. Troopships were often floating hellholes chartered from private shippers, so in 1866 the Royal Navy built its own, paid for by the Indian Government, each displaying the Star of India on its bows. The new vessels were part of the maritime revolution of the 1860s, when steam began to replace sail as the means of propulsion. Five troopers of a similar design with sails and engines, the *Crocodile, Euphrates, Jumna, Malabar (V)* and *Serapis* plied the sea route from Britain to Suez and India for the next three decades. They were as familiar to thousands of soldiers in those days, as the Boeings and Airbuses are to the shopping warriors of Bermuda today.

In 1897, HMS *Malabar V* was sent to Bermuda as the station ship, being renamed HMS *Terror*, which turned at its mooring below the Dockyard Parsonage for several decades. In 1919, the vessel was sold out of service and its original name was transferred to the Commissioner's House, which became HMS Malabar VI until 1951 when the Royal Navy downsized the Bermuda station.

A number of Bermudian ladies still remember attending balls at this Malabar as young girls. During the 1939–45 war, the House served as a vital interception centre of submarine radio traffic that covered the North Atlantic with Halifax to the north and Derby to the east.

Now restored by the Maritime Museum, the Commissioner's House preserves the naval heritage of those, including many Bermudians, who served at HMS Malabar and the Bermuda Dockyard for 180 years, until its closure in 1995.

EDWARD HARRIS

Outrigging a mahogany tree

Soon after I began my doctoral studies in archaeology in the dampness of London, the late and well know Headmaster of Whitney Academy, Ron Cripps Brown, Owen Darrell and others of the Rotary International Clubs in Bermuda, encouraged me to apply for a Rotary Graduate Fellowship. Perhaps its most outstanding achievement is somewhat under-sung: the scholarship programme of Rotary International has been sending worthy students around the world for many decades, a cultural exchange which has brought nothing but benefit to all concerned.

So it was that I found myself in 1977 at the Australian National University in Canberra for a year of research, in the heat of gum tree forests abounding in kangaroo. It appears that my scholastic skills were not the top issue with members of the selection committee at the Department of Prehistory, who had made their choice on the assumption that coming from Bermuda I would be a cricketer and make a good addition to the departmental team. Much to their dismay, my utter incompetence at the sport was demonstrated when I perceived a red cannonball speeding my way and retreated from the field, discretion being the better part of valour, if not cricket.

The Department of Prehistory did some academic work between cricket matches and some of the research took place in New Guinea, after Greenland, the largest island in the world. Politically, New Guinea is divided in half, with the western section being a reluctant part of Indonesia and the eastern an independent state as of 1975. It was my privilege to join two research projects in Papua New Guinea, one to the highlands near Mount Hagen and the other to the Admiralty Islands. In the highlands, we were looking for traces of early agricultural systems and on the islands for remains of prehistoric settlement.

Papua New Guinea is an extraordinary place, significantly divided between the plains of the coast and the highlands of the interior by very mountainous and unstable limestone geology. There are still areas of the country where the only way in is by foot or helicopter, so difficult is the terrain for the building and maintenance of roads. People have settled the coastal regions for thousands of years, and New Guinea was a part of a land bridge for humans migrating into Australia in prehistory across the Torres Strait.

Until the late 1920s, the highlands were thought to be uninhabited.

Typical dugout with outrigger under sail

Owner with finished hull

Harris and boat tree stump

When the first planes arrived in the country at that time, a couple of Irishmen from Port Moresby, the capital, were able to fly over the intervening mountain range. From the air, they saw that the great valleys of the highland plateau were full of people and gardens, an astounding discovery for the larger world. They moved to the highlands and married into the local community, establishing several dynasties and developing gold mines.

From the viewpoint of anthropology, New Guinea was a gold mine of ethnicities for its difficult landscape, causing the separation of peoples over time, resulted in the creation of some 700 languages and as many different societies over 60,000 years.

When we were in the Admiralty Islands, much of our travel was in dugout canoes, with decks, sails and outriggers, though outboard engines were also coming into vogue. We visited many islands where that was the only mode of transport to the outer world, excepting the occasional motorboat of missionaries. On one occasion, we travelled in such a boat, where the drinking of tea put us into the heathen category, to say nothing of imbibing stronger liquids.

In one coastal area, we ventured into the interior with villagers who were making a dugout canoe. The process started high in the forest with the selection of a large mahogany tree. The majestic tree was cut down by hand and roughly half the length of its trunk was removed. In a forest clearing, the digging-out began, using a few iron hand tools, some of which, like the adze, are traditional boatbuilding implements. In earlier times, all the tools would have been made with stone cutting heads.

The half-finished hull was then hauled out of the forest to the shore of the village, where the final excavation of the tree took place. For extra support, "ribs" were sculpted within, but in the end the canoe was only a single piece of wood deriving its stability from the strength of the tree it once was. In this instance, the dugout canoe was intended as a float for a deck, with an outrigger added for sea-going capabilities.

It was vessels of this type that carried early peoples across the seas of New Guinea and throughout the south and west Pacific. Bermuda was not settled until Europeans began to roam the ocean seas, for the technology of such large sailing canoes was not available to the early peoples of the eastern coasts of the Americas.

Ferrying the legend of Venturilla

Spanish Point was a place of mystery and endless pleasure in the sea-swept days of our youth as members of the numerous Harris family. Residing nearby, we spent most of the summer in the shallow, warm and sparkling waters of the small beaches on the north side of the peninsula. In the bay to the south was the mysterious wreckage we now know was the remains of the great and first Royal Naval Floating Dock, HMS *Bermuda*. Little did we know that we walked and played over the campsite of the first recorded "negro" to visit Bermuda, along with his crewmates for whom Spanish Point is named. Venturilla was his name and he has now been ferried into present memory by the naming of a new fast shuttle boat in his honour.

Of the man himself, little is know and had he not been attacked by the night-travelling Bermuda cahows, his presence here may have gone unrecorded. His name is Spanish and likely to be a derivation of ventura, for venture or adventure. He may have been a slave or a free man; he may have been a Moor from the north or an African from south of the Sahara. "Negro" is the translation of his person given in the main source available, so we must await some scholarly look at the original script of the diary of Diego Ramirez, Venturilla's captain, to agree absolutely on his origins.

As far as we will probably ever know, Venturilla was the first African to set foot in Bermuda. If we judge him not on the colour of his skin but on the content of his character, he has another claim to fame, for he and his shipmates helped to create the first detailed map of Bermuda, published here in colour for the first time. They also gave rise to the oldest place name in Bermuda, that of Spanish Point.

> **Going to the rescue, his shipmates found Venturilla under a Hitchcock-like attack of birds, which were attracted to the light of the lantern. The men resolved the matter by clubbing to death some 500 cahows**

Before we look at the map in detail, we can recap the adventure that brought Venturilla to Bermuda for an enforced three-week visit in 1603. In that year, probably out of Havana, the small fleet of Don Luis de Cordoba was assailed by storms in the Florida Strait and four ships were lost. Another vessel under Captain Diego Ramirez then suffered misfortune when it struck the reef on the north side of Bermuda. Damaged but not sinking, the ship made its way over the reef and found a place of refuge in the Great Sound, most likely in the bay at Spanish Point, the last home of the floating dock.

While repairs were underway, Ramirez and some of the men explored the island in a small boat. On one occasion at night, the rudder broke and Venturilla, possibly being a shipwright, was sent ashore with a lantern to cut a piece of replacement cedar. Soon after, he cried out in such a manner that Ramirez thought he was being carried off by the devils said to inhabit Bermuda. Going to his rescue, they found Venturilla under a Hitchcock-like attack of birds, which were attracted to the light of the lantern. The men resolved the matter by clubbing to death some 500 cahows, starting the species on the road to possible extinction by this and subsequent massacres ("The birds were so plentiful that 4,000 could be taken in a single bag"). Their provisions being lost in striking the reef, the cahows, wild pigs and numerous species of fish provided the hungry mariners with a full larder when they left Bermuda.

The explorers gave a fulsome description of Bermuda, even noting the presence of tobacco plants, cultivated by some earlier shipwrecked mariners. The island was covered with cedar and palmetto forests,

Spanish Point from the air—Venturilla's likely landing place

Cross, or Magazine, Island, now part of the Dockyard breakwater

EDWARD HARRIS

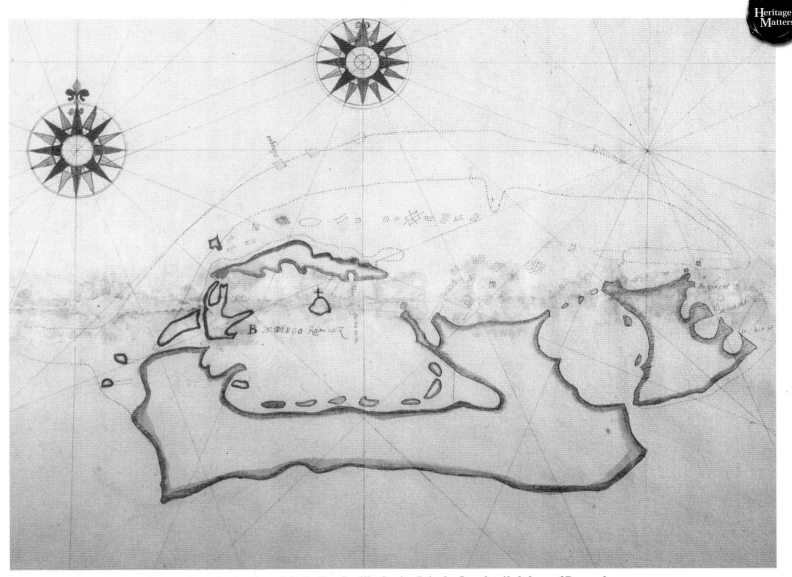

The Diego Ramirez map of 1603, from the Archive of the Indies, Seville, Spain. It is the first detailed chart of Bermuda

with some other evergreens. The large herds of swine had made highways leading to watering holes, along which the bark of the palmettos was worn through, being used by the pigs as backscratchers. Crows were so abundant that they used the mariners' heads and arms as perches. The absence of mosquitoes was made up for by the presence of innumerable flies.

The travels of the mariners around Bermuda are recorded in their map, which has one glaring exception—the absence of Harrington Sound. This suggests it may have been landlocked at that time, or was simply not observed in any part. Castle and St George's Harbours are merged into one, with indentations such as Tobacco Bay on the north and eastern coast of St. George's Island exaggerated. The bay at Spanish Point is also larger than life, as it was there that Ramirez's ship was probably beached for repairs.

The Bermuda fast ferry commemorating Venturilla

On an island between Spanish Point and the dockyard a cross is shown, with the name Diego Ramirez below. Ramirez placed the cross there with instructions for later mariners on the location of fresh water. Later on it became associated with a treasure story whereby the cross, lined up from Spanish Point, indicated the buried loot at a place near Westgate prison. The three Dockyard islands of Watford, Boaz and Ireland are also charted. The main island of Great

Bermuda is considerable distorted, but after three weeks of drinking palmetto berry juice, the result is nonetheless the remarkable and earliest surviving detailed chart of Bermuda, 100 years after its discovery.

Four hundred and two years later, Venturilla would undoubtedly be pleased to see his namesake ferrying passengers past his old home at Spanish Point every day of the year, but in the evenings, he would perhaps wonder where all the cahows have gone.

Architects of our own demise

Changing streetscape of Front Street

Trimingham's, which is no more, is still with us, at least in the form of the bright orange beacon of commerce at the head of Front Street [later demolished in January, 2007]. Disquiet and sadness attended the passing of its soul and controversy seems now certain to dog its death. Some foreign elements are intent upon the destruction of one of the greatest symbols of Bermuda's tourism heyday, its very façade and sidewalk. Xenophobia, one of our fondest addictions and curses, arises from its latest short slumber. First they took our bank and now they are taking our shopping mall. Do they not know that we cannot wear money, even as Bermuda shorts?

But, my fellow countryfolk, we are the architects of our own demise, not the HSBC/Bank of Bermuda. As Jonathan Dyer suggested in a letter to an editor, we are the ones who have sold our souls—and cheaply at that. However, some are banking on the Bank to do the right thing in the end and increase the share value of Bermuda's built heritage by designing a good building for posterity.

Demise is an ancient legal term for the transfer or conveyance of property with all rights and privileges. It also signifies the immediate "transfer of sovereignty" upon the death of the monarch, so that there is no hiatus in the functioning of the state. Thus it is closely associated with the concept of endings, passings and outright death. So we can speak of the demise of tourism, as the cynics (or perhaps realists) do,

or of the demise of the unique heritage of this paradise on earth. A place where a lower salary is at least five to 10,000 times greater than the one dollar a day that half the population of the world lives on. Yet we are disconsolate that we can no longer shop at Trimingham's.

Trimingham's is symbolic of the demise of tourism and the continuing assault and decay of the built heritage of the island. On one hand, it represented the fine shopping that once obtained on the island and which kept the well-heeled well heeled, well dressed and returning to Bermuda. On the other hand, its headquarters building was a part of the outstanding heritage streetscape of the City of Hamilton. The coming wrecker's ball represents not the proverbial

The two facades of Trimingham's. The last incarnation was demolished in January 2007, making way for a new building

nail in the coffin, but the oblivion of the crematorium, where there is not a bone, not a single tooth left to represent what once existed. There will be nothing for the archivist, the archaeologist or the visitor to see, nor a vestige from which an earlier glory of architecture can be imagined.

In the City of Hamilton, the demise, the transfer of sovereignty, of its historic architecture began decades ago. It was accelerated with the large pots of gold that the tourism trade produced, a trade that had its very foundations in the surviving historic architecture of Bermuda that had created an ambience found in few other places. One of the pots of gold created the multi-storey car park thing on top of Trimingham's several decades ago. Those who made that glass house—architects and owners—dare not throw stones at the new design some people are banking on.

Against this transfer, the then-new Department of Planning proved to be a paper tiger. Perhaps in response to the loss of preservation sovereignty, the Bermuda National Trust was established some 30 years ago. What careful government should have done, the National Trust has attempted to do throughout Bermuda. That it has failed catastrophically in the City of Hamilton is not so much a matter of blame for the largely volunteer organisation, but the major indicator of the abdication of the powers that be and the powers with the money. They failed or refused to see any value in the preservation of the architectural fabric that was a vital thread that once made our tourism cloth so vibrant and successful. We sold out our real "international business" of tourism long before the others of that

name came here less than 25 years ago. Look in the mirror when you seek to blame the new outsiders.

Look at the interior views of Messrs. Child's and Trimingham's stores at the close of the Victorian era. The last store to have anything like the charm encapsulated in these "show rooms" was probably Peniston Brown's: they have probably thrown the baby out with the perfume by now as well. Look at the verandas of Trimingham's in 1898 and compare to the concrete structure now awaiting its death: what on earth happened? Why is there but a few Trader's Gates (restored by Butterfield Bank) that attempt to retain the Bermudian architectural idiom, for our own sense of identity and for the edification of our visitors? Look at the streetscape on Front Street from 1898 and from last week (death awaits the photographer who dares to stand in the middle of the road to get exactly the same view) and you see a great crane, the harbinger of the chaos and lack of charm of international-style architecture, when dumped into historic Bermuda.

I cannot say that you can have it all as this is home and I do not wish to leave, nor to be forced out by the demise of our built heritage, given by our forebears. Perhaps I can ask the new corporations to do what many Bermudians have not done: find some good architects who do not wish to advance the demise of the outstanding local vernacular and who will design office blocks that fit the land in which they are to be permanent citizens. We want our buildings to speak Bermudian, not some international dialect. Perhaps it is no accident that many older Bermudians are incapable of pronouncing the word "architect" correctly.

Charming interiors of two 1890s shops: Edwin T. Child's showroom and at right, Trimingham's

Five Bermudian lives torpedoed

The sun from the sea first touches Bermuda at St. David's Head, the easternmost part of the island. There, under the protective guns of an old battery, the Bermuda Government has erected a monument to local inhabitants lost at sea. A purpose of such a monument is to remind us of the lives that the great forces of nature or the destructive hand of man interrupted irrevocably and whose only grave is that of the sea.

There are those who go down through foolishness, who test the mighty ocean with arrogance or inadequate implements. Most, however, meet their end while undertaking the duties of the mariner on a day that went wrong. Others reach an uninvited but honourable fate, as did five Bermudians whose lives were literally torpedoed in the line of military duties. They are recorded in Bermuda's Roll of Honour of those killed in action in the world war of 1939–45 and honoured annually on Remembrance Day.

Three of these men served in the Merchant Marine, the movers of essential cargoes who suffered considerable losses through U-boat attacks. Another served in one of His Majesty's warships and the last was coming home when his ship was sunk. Perhaps their names will be recorded along with the civilian losses at the St. David's monument.

DOUGLAS WILLIAM HOWARD HUTCHINGS was lost on January 16, 1941. He was an oiler, whose first job was in the engine room of the *Queen of Bermuda*, but had transferred to another vessel. At the time of his death, *Queen* was on duty in the Falkland Islands far to the south. According to Billy McGee, who had an excellent website on the Merchant Navy, there were two British vessels sunk on January 16, 1941, the *Zealandic* and the *Oropesa*.

Both were attacked off Rockall, some 300 miles from Iceland and Ireland on the route from the North Sea to the Atlantic. The cargo ship *Zealandic* was lost with all hands and *Oropesa*, a passenger liner, lost 105 crew and passengers, with 143 being rescued. Given that he was originally on a passenger liner, it is possible that Hutchings was lost on the *Oropesa*. It was sunk by U-96, a boat familiar to most through its incarnation as the lead actor in the outstanding film, *Das Boot*. Of the 40,000 mariners of the U-boat fleets, 30,000 did not return from sea.

HOWARD SINCLAIR BURGESS was a fireman and trimmer and with 28 others on the *Henri Mory* was lost on April 26, 1941. The *Henri Mory* had sailed with a cargo of iron ore from Pepel and Freetown in Sierra Leone for Barrow in Scotland. One source suggests that the ship came to Bermuda and it is possible that Burgess joined the vessel and his fate here. The *Henri Mory* had left Convoy SL-68 and was travelling independently when the ship was torpedoed by U-110 in the North Atlantic. The U-110 had a very short career of only two sailings and was sunk a few weeks after the *Henri Mory* went down. The boat became famous for it remained afloat long enough for the British to board it and remove an Enigma code machine and many secret documents.

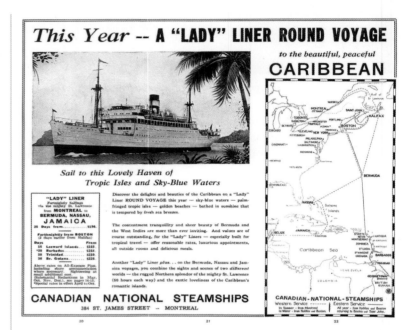

Pages from brochures for the Lady Boats

LIEUT. CECIL JOHN GREENWAY WRIGHT was serving in the Royal Naval Volunteer Reserve on HMS *Dunedin* when the vessel was torpedoed on November 24, 1941. He was one of the 419 men lost, only 67 of the crew surviving. In 1940, *Dunedin* had been

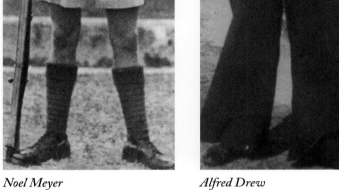

Noel Meyer   Alfred Drew

A Second World War convoy in the Great Sound at Bermuda

Cecil Wright   Howard Burgess   Douglas Hutchings

Capt. Richard Zapp on the U-66 and USS Buckley, *damaged by ramming*

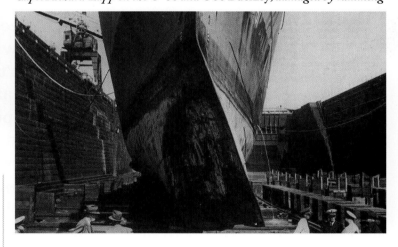

posted to the America and West Indies Station at Bermuda and thereafter was on the South Atlantic Station. While pursuing enemy surface ships in those waters, the *Dunedin* was sent to an oceanic grave by U-124, halfway between Sierre Leone and Brazil.

NOEL LUMLEY MEYER was returning to Bermuda via Canada after service with the Royal Air Force. He was travelling on the *Lady Hawkins*, one of the famous "Lady Boats" that had served Bermuda and the West Indies for several decades. The ship was torpedoed on January 19, 1942 south of Boston by U-66 under the command of Richard Zapp, with the loss of 255 souls. Meyer was last seen helping survivors into lifeboats, 71 persons later being rescued. The USS *Buckley* sank the U-66 by ramming on May 6, 1944.

ALFRED DAVID DREWSBURY DREW remains an enigmatic merchant mariner. While he is recorded on the Bermuda Roll of Honour, neither his date nor place of death is presently known. At the beginning of the Second World War in 1939, he was a young man of 20 years. It is said that he volunteered for convoy service to

Britain and was lost when his ship was torpedoed. His name is not recorded on the lists of the Commonwealth War Graves Commission. This suggests that he died on his first voyage, before his name could be recorded officially as a member of his ship's crew. Further research may finally complete the story of this young Bermudian lost at sea in the line of duty.

Like a stone thrown into the sea, a sinking vessel creates but a few ripples that are soon lost to sight, as is the ship itself. The loss of its crew makes destructive emotional waves that resound down through the years in the lives and memory of family and friends left behind. Memory itself cannot escape the shipwreck of time, unless we hold it firm in archival records and built monuments. We make these memory banks to respect the dead and honour their contributions to the present, especially those who gave their lives in the line of duty.

Guns out of sight at Scaur Hill Fort

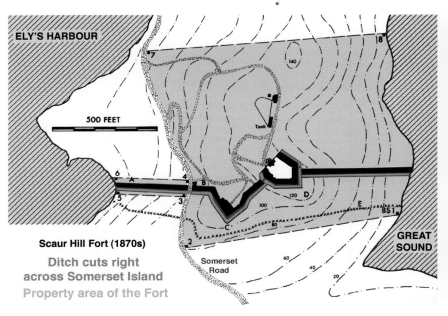

A map of the ditch across Somerset

Scaur Hill Fort from the air

Somerset Bridge is a useless monument, at least in military terms. Its drawbridge can let the masts of small sailing boats pass through, but with today's thunderous traffic it is unlikely to be so used ever again. Militarily, it is no drawbridge at all, unlike those at the Dockyard that left a gaping hole in the road when withdrawn. Yet Somerset Bridge was a critical point for any army attacking the Dockyard, as it was the only bridge from the island of Bermuda to Somerset.

With the longer range of guns in the 1850s, it was necessary to prevent an invading army from reaching into Somerset, from where its guns could shell Watford, Boaz and Ireland Island with impunity. It is possible that Somerset Bridge may have been built as a military drawbridge at this time, but no such mention is recorded. Rather, the procedure was probably to destroy the bridge by hand, or shell it into oblivion with the guns of the new fort on Scaur Hill, less than a mile to the north.

The enemy would have heard its guns but would have been sightless, for the cannon were mounted on the new Moncrieff "disappearing carriage." According to artillery historian Collin Carpenter FSA, we have at Scaur Hill Fort the last know remains of Capt. Moncrieff's smallest disappearing carriage. Pieces at other local forts were thrown out, for no one knew at the time what they were.

The disappearing gun was emplaced at the forts of the "Prospect Position," being Langton, Prospect and Hamilton, and at Scaur Hill. This type of cannon was for land use, the coastal guns of the period being of larger dimensions to fire upon iron warships. Fort Langton, demolished in 1984, was unique having both coastal guns facing the

Now you see it, now you don't: the amazing disappearing cannon carriage defending Dockyard

South Channel to Dockyard and land guns fronting the valleys of Devonshire.

Scaur Hill Fort is a monument of some architectural interest, for it displays in stone and concrete the great change taking place in the design of fortifications in the last quarter of the 19th century. Until that time, forts were buildings for offensive action that could also be defended. Forts Hamilton, Prospect and Langton, though built at the same time as Scaur Hill, were good examples of the defendable fort, the last of their kind. The two forts in the west, Whale Bay and Scaur, have features of defence, but these are mostly shrunken versions of the original. The idea of a fort was being replaced by simple gun positions with little defensive architecture, such as seen at St. David's Battery, home of the Bermuda Militia Artillery in the first half of the 20th century.

The ditch at Scaur Hill Fort is the longest in Bermuda. It starts on the eastern side of Somerset Island, runs around the southern edge of the fort, proceeding westward across the road and downhill to Ely's Harbour. A wooden bridge on Somerset Road once spanned the ditch. On the north side of the ditch, soldiers would have been manned a wide bank to shoot towards the approaching enemy. Over their heads, the two cannon of the Fort would fire into the peninsula that ends at Somerset Bridge and beyond, demolishing such buildings as the "Hitching Post," if it had existed.

The operation of the disappearing carriage is shown here in a model that is part of the Collin and Jenny Carpenter Collection at the Bermuda Maritime Museum. In this instance, Collin—nicknamed "Guns" by Bermudians—was so excited by the parts of the Moncreiff

The gun and parts of its carriage at Scaur Hill

carriage he saw here in 1985 that he made this working model.

When the gun is fired, the force of the shot pushes the barrel and carriage down into the gun emplacement. The gun is loaded in that depressed position, while the enemy is looking from whence the firing came, hopefully without success. Once reloaded, a latch is released and a five-ton counter-weight throws the gun back into its elevated position over the rampart. The gun is fired and again disappears from view.

Some years ago, the then curator at Scaur Hill, Lance Furbert, found the cheeks of the carriages in the bushes at the fort. The counterweights were then found on the Hamilton docks and through the courtesy of the then-manager, Mike Lohan, Stevedoring Services were relieved of several of these artifacts, which were taken to Scaur Hill Fort for posterity.

Times change, enemies come and go. A clear and present danger in the later 1800s, it is now hard to imagine that an American enemy would have come marching through Southampton, southern Sandys and into Somerset to attack the Royal Naval Dockyard, after a landing on the South Shore beaches. To prevent such an invasion and American occupation of Bermuda, seven new forts were built here in the late Victorian period and a number were rearmed with advanced weapons. The system appears to have worked.

Thanks to the enemy of old, a mere 700 miles to the west, Bermuda has an outstanding array of military architecture and artillery. If we would but care more for these monuments, we might invite more Americans to our shores in their modern invasion in the gentler guise of friendly visitors.

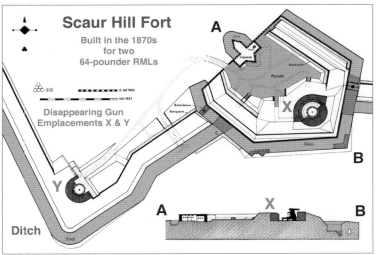

A plan of Scaur Hill Fort

A model by Collin "Guns" Carpenter of a gun on its Moncreiff disappearing carriage

St. George: heritage heart of Bermuda

On a good day 100,000 years ago, the prevailing westerly winds would have washed over Bermuda without interference from any living thing, except for the few true indigenous locals. The cahows and longtails nested in peace, skinks basked in the tropic sun and the palmetto and Bermuda cedar held sway over a landscape yet to be blighted by casuarinas, pepper and laurel trees. Later on, no natives of the two great continents to the west and the islands to the south had boats that could traverse the Gulf Stream, nor navigation skills to locate the oceanic dot of Bermuda. No St. Brendan, no Vikings or raiders from the north fetched this far south and the natural life of the island continued as it had for eons until a fateful day in 1505.

On that date yet to be determined exactly, Juan de Bermúdez was sailing home to Europe on one of his many trans-Atlantic voyages as a pilot in the Spanish service. By choice or accident, Juan had picked up the best east-bound track to the Old World by sailing north from the Florida Straits with the Gulf Stream and turning right in the vicinity of Bermuda to pick up the trade winds that would push his vessel home across the ocean sea. Thus it was that 500 years ago, 64 degrees West and 32 degrees North became known as Las Bermudas, in honour of its first human discoverer, the pilot from Palos. The first record of his discovery appeared in 1511 when the position of Bermuda was published in a sea chart of the Western Atlantic. To human consciousness the island was so born, if not inhabited for over a century, not by the nation of its discoverer but by England, its enemy in the American enterprises.

Before settlement occurred, the ecological devastation of Bermuda had begun in earnest, for the Spanish had a habit of infesting islands they passed with fast food products in the event of shipwrecking. These were pigs, or more exactly, boars of the wild order, complete with tusks and expert rooting capacities. When passing, the boars would be tossed overboard and being the best of swimmers and good floaters would make their way ashore, to multiple, occupy and devastate the earth. These four-legged bulldozers would have cut swaths of

Dramatic whaling diorama in the new "Gateway to Bermuda" exhibit

destruction throughout Bermuda, eating every egg and baby of the ground-nesting cahows and long-tails. Skinks would have provided a choice desert and the pears of the prickly cactus would have served for a change of palate. As is known from a celebrated murder case in Britain some years ago, they would have eaten people also if the opportunity had arisen.

The delicate environment was further unbalanced in 1609, when the *Sea Venture* ended up on the rocks at the east end, instead of resting at anchor in the tidewaters off the first English American settlement at Jamestown, Virginia. James Fort, as it was originally, was established in 1607 and the 1609 fleet of nine ships was bringing more settlers and supplies but met with a hurricane. Eight of the vessels, including the *Virginia*, the first ship built by the English in America the previous year, made it through, but the *Sea Venture* was seriously damaged. Leaking badly, the end was near when the weather cleared and the ship's complement found themselves stuck on a reef a stone's throw from a beach, later called St. Catherine's, at Bermuda. Everyone made it ashore and this classic tale of shipwreck is said to have been the foundation of *The Tempest* by Shakespeare. Making a couple of small boats and leaving a dissident behind, the settlers finally reached Jamestown in July 1610, with boars and salted cahows aboard, the bones of the latter being found in recent archaeological digs in Virginia.

This sojourn led to the permanent human settlement of Bermuda by the English in late July 1612, some 60 souls venturing across the Atlantic to an uncertain future on the Isle of Devils. They founded the first English town in the Americas, apparently called "New London," but St. George's soon became its accepted name. Until 1815, it was the capital and heritage heart of Bermuda.

In 2000, the town and the fortifications of St. George's Parish became Bermuda's World Heritage Site, as designated by UNESCO, in the company of some 700 sites worldwide. While deserving of that appellation due to the age and extraordinary architecture of St. George's and the fortifications, it remains to be seen if Bermuda

The Penno's Wharf Queen's Warehouse building in its new incarnation as the St. George's World Heritage Centre

Detail of a 1620s St. George's town model now on display

The great wheel for hoisting cargo has been retained in the centre

merits the continuation of that honour, for much needs to be done in maintaining and upgrading our World Heritage Site.

The establishment of the St. George's Foundation is one of the bright lights on the horizon in this respect. Having raised considerable funds from the public with recent major support from the Government, the Foundation is hard at work building a heritage and information centre at Penno's Wharf on the west side of St. George's. The Centre is housed in the old Queen's Warehouse, a restored 19th-Century

building near the cruise ship terminal at Tiger Bay.

The Centre, with its developing exhibits and educational facilities, is intended to serve as the gateway for tours of St. George's, as well as leading visitors to heritage destinations throughout Bermuda. Being the seat of Bermuda's settlement and containing such a wealth of monuments, St. George's will always be the heritage heart of Bermuda. The new developments there should to be welcomed and encouraged by all in Bermuda.

Hogging the money at Castle Island

A Hog sixpence found at King's Castle

Malcolm Williams and Leanora Stovel-Smith of the BMA with a Hog shilling

As we contemplate the 500th anniversary of the discovery of Bermuda by the Spanish pilot and first transporter of African slaves to the New World, Juan de Bermúdez, the most resonant icon of our early days would appear to be the pig, or hog. In another article I have mistakenly referred to such animals collectively as boars, but as some appreciate, this applies only to the male of the species.

Pigs were the only large animals found at Bermuda until settlement in 1612. They came to populate the island after its discovery in 1505, either swimming from wrecked ships or being sent ashore from Spanish vessels. One of the first pictures of Bermuda, a water-coloured map attributed to Sir George Somers in 1609, has a central vignette of men and dogs hunting pigs in Warwick. Some of the hogs were taken to Jamestown, Virginia, the following summer, helping to save the starving colonists in that first permanent English settlement in the Americas, Bermuda being the second. So the pigs from Bermuda might be said to have saved the fledgling US of A.

In April 1612, the shareholders of the Virginia Company were making preparations to settle Bermuda and had appointed Richard Moore to be their first governor. The *Plough* was being outfitted, but would not sail until July "to go directly to the Islands without stopping anywhere else." Upon arrival, Moore was to find "a suitable place to settle [St. George's], to place a fort, build a storehouse" and make houses for people on the basis of "1 rood to each single man and 2 roods to each married couple." By modern condo standards, this would be about 80 dwellings per acre.

From the industry of the settlers in agriculture, half of the produce would accrue to the shareholders and the other half to the people themselves. Men working for the Company would be paid "at the Governor's discretion up to 20d per day for a workman and 12d for a labourer for which a coin shall be sent to the Governor as soon as possible." This was to be the first coinage made by the English for their overseas empire, but Governor Moore never saw any of it.

In 1616 a new governor, the first of the Bermuda Tuckers, one Daniel, was sent out to the island. He was under instructions to do a deal with labourers whereby they would be paid by credits with the Company, such paper profits being the difference between the cost of their provisions and the sale of their production. Any worker who did not want this bookkeeping arrangement could opt out, to "be paid in base coin which will be sent out."

The copper coinage duly arrived, later "silvered" to improve on its baseness and overcome its dislike by the settlers. Even that was a bit of a sham, for Bermudian conservator Heidi Leseur, when at the British Museum, showed it to be coated in tin. The 200-odd settlers received the base coinage with derision. Governor Nathaniel Butler (1619) describes it as having a "huge stamp upon it on the one side (in memory it should seem of the great number of wild swine found upon the islands at their first discovery)," and says it was, "in a scoff, termed by the people hog-money."

The coins, of which less than 100 may still exist, had on the obverse the impression of a pig surrounded by the legend, SOMMER ILANDS. On the reverse was an artist's bastardised view of a ship. It came in four denominations: the twopence, threepence, sixpence and twelvepence or shilling. Derided by the first Bermudians, it was probably often discarded. Someone, however, out on one of the lonely islands of Castle Harbour, was hogging the money, for 19 pieces of it were found in an archaeological excavation in 1993.

In that year, Bermuda Maritime Museum and the College of William & Mary were studying the first forts on the island and excavations had begun at the King's Castle on the headland of Castle Island, one of the most evocative places in Bermuda. A ditch was discovered to the rear of the fort and the Captain's House (1621), the first house to be made of Bermuda stone. From the time of its creation, the inhabitants of the fort and house had thrown their kitchen refuse into the ditch and thousands of fish bones attest to a healthy diet. Mixed in with the food waste were pottery shards and 19 pieces of Hog Money.

The coins were probably in a purse or on a shelf and were tossed out with the trash "in a scoff" against the new Bermuda Company's introduction of a coinage with none but local value, much like the Bermuda dollar today. In those times, the Spanish dollar held sway internationally, much as the U.S. dollar does today.

The first coin found is thought to be the finest example of Hog Money and all are on display at the Commissioner's House in the Bank of Bermuda Foundation's coinage exhibit. By happenstance it was discovered just as the then-president of the Bermuda National Trust and *The Royal Gazette* editor, David L. White, visited the excavations.

The last coin was found in 1993 by budding archaeologists from the Bermuda Monetary Authority, which acts as custodians with the Museum for this unique collection of the island's first coinage. If nothing else, the coinage commemorates the arrival of the pig at Bermuda 500 years ago. Therefore is not the old swine, if extinct, more indigenous than the rest of us?

The mistaken idea of a causeway to nowhere

We have a great capacity to delude ourselves and to accept as fact much of what is served up to us. This is especially so in historical matters, where our critical facilities have not been well honed and suppositions become legend and then fact. One still repeated fact is that the Dockyard is built of imported stone, "brought out in ballast," a phrase which for some reason catches people's imagination. As any visitor to Home Depot or Wal-Mart will know, very little comes to Bermuda in ballast, now or then. Cargo is always number one on the manifest, for goodies, not rocks, and is what is desirable in the Isles of Rest. The Dockyard, as John Burland told me 25 years ago, is made of Bermuda stone and "don't you believe what everyone else will tell you: that it is from England." Of course, I did not believe him until I sent some samples to the Geological Museum in London. The reply somewhat embarrassingly said: "the samples are not English, but match perfectly with specimens of Bermuda limestone in our collections."

Trying to change such set ideas is like rolling a pile of jail-nuts up Lighthouse Hill; while some are being moved up, the others are running back down to the South Shore Road. One such wayward fact is the description of a photograph of the gunpowder magazine on Agar's Island as "the Causeway to St. George's under construction," so published on a number of occasions, despite attempted corrections to the contrary. The photograph shows black workmen standing on the walls and vaulted roofs of a structure under construction. In the background is a narrow body of water with land rising behind, a configuration that cannot be matched at the Causeway, built in 1871. Sizing up the width of the structure, this Causeway would have been ready for autobahn status upon its completion, with three lanes of traffic in each direction.

The walls are not continuous, which is what would be expected if the rooms were tunnels to allow the waters of Castle Harbour to wash through into Ferry Reach. Rather, the division between the walls is a corridor. The roofs of the rooms are arched and made of a half-dozen courses of brick, which would be overkill for a horse and carriage roadway of the 1870s. No hurricane would have ever budged this structure, as Fabian did so effectively to the real Causeway.

This picture records the only known view of the construction of one of Bermuda's forts and magazines in the great rebuilding after the late 1860s. It also records that Bermudians were carrying out the building of those structures, under the supervision of the Royal Engineers. Given the geography and architecture captured in this early photograph, the building can only be the huge Rifled Muzzle Loader powder magazine on Agar's Island, which forms the north side of Two Rock Passage into Hamilton Harbour.

In the later 1850s, the English developed a rear-loading cannon, for better sealing and effective use of the propellant. It also had a barrel with twisted rifling to impart a spin to the new elongated projectiles, a major departure from the round cannonball of previous centuries.

The 1870s photograph of the Agar's Island magazines under construction. Below: two RMLs discovered at the Maritime Museum

These guns revolutionised artillery and began the modern arms race. Their existence led to the development of iron ships and to the remodelling of old forts and the building of new designs to match the increased firepower of rifled artillery. Once again, Bermuda was in for an economic bonanza created by the construction of military works.

The new gun was called a Rifled Breech Loader, or RBL, and was made of wrought iron. A fundamental design flaw led to wrought iron Rifled Muzzle Loaders, or RMLs. Bermuda possesses four RBLs and 46 RMLs; several of the latter were found under the grass of the Keep Yard at the Maritime Museum some years ago.

During the RBL and RML bonanza at Bermuda, six new forts were constructed and six remodelled. The military provided Bermudians with a number of construction extravaganzas, beginning after the American Revolutionary War in the 1790s. The building of the Dockyard and forts took 50 years from 1809 onwards. No sooner had those ended, new works of the RBL guns commenced in the 1860s. The invention of gun steel led to further moneymakers, including St. David's Battery, in the late 1890s. Dockyard was expanded and from this time many men of the West Indies came to work in the major construction market; their descendants are here today. The final military contribution to the economic wellbeing of Bermuda came with the building of the US bases in the early 1940s.

Two free standing RBL/RML gunpowder magazines were built in the 1870s, one on Boaz Island and the other on Agar's Island. The commodious magazines and light passages in the Agar's building were used to create the first aquarium in Bermuda in the 1920s. An explosives magazine it was first, a watery attraction secondly, but a causeway never.

Bermuda archaeology finally comes of age

Children like change and the unexpected and Sister Jean de Chantal Kennedy was therefore a likeable person. Amidst the chaos of a Mount Saint Agnes Academy classroom and projectiles from peashooters and rubber-band slingshots, Sister Jean could be counted on to deviate from the stated curriculum. One day when English was to be taught, we were informed about dining table etiquette and on other occasions, we were treated to a rundown on local historical figures from her research in the local archives. Ahead of her times, Sister Jean, the author of a half-dozen books on Bermuda, was also interested in applying archaeological methods to extract more history from the land.

In the late 1960s, Sister Jean and I looked into excavating a small fort in Smith's Parish, then standing in a wilderness, now surrounded by houses. In the early 1970s, however, it was Dr. David Fleming, a Bermudian scholar, who carried out the first archaeological "dig" in Bermuda in the cellar of the Tucker House in St. George's. So it was on a National Trust site that archaeology was introduced to Bermuda. Since then, archaeology has come of age in Bermuda and this fact is expressed in an encompassing exhibition on the subject,

Archaeologists at work at an excavation at Port Royal golf course

temporarily on show at the Masterworks Rose Garden Gallery at Camden. A note of thanks is due to Masterworks and its Director, Tom Butterfield, for allowing the display in their domain.

The exhibit is the brainchild of Richard Lowry, Bermudian archaeologist, and he and his committee, including marine archaeologist Dr. Clifford Smith, brought together the Bermuda National Trust, the Bermuda Maritime Museum, the Bermuda Underwater Exploration Institute and the Department of Conservation Services to accomplish the goal of presenting archaeological research in the island to the

public. An educational supplement edited by Jennifer Hind appeared in *The Royal Gazette* and the projects received financial support from the Bank of Bermuda Foundation, Butterfield Bank, Ministry of the Environment, ACE Foundation, XL Foundation, PartnerRe, MaxRe, and RenaissanceRe. Paul Shapiro and Rosemary Jones of Brimstone Media wrote and designed the exhibit.

Archaeology is a scientific discipline that is the only way in which history found in the ground, on underwater sites and in standing buildings can be correctly examined and recorded. No other discipline perhaps has done so much to change our view of history and our place on Earth. For all human culture before or without written language, archaeology provides the only means by which such earlier peoples can be understood and appreciated for their role in the worldwide development of human beings. It seems almost impossible to imagine a world without the epic discoveries of Early Man in Africa, the Inca or Mayan empires of the Americas, Henry VIII's flagship *Mary Rose* or the terracotta armies of a Chinese emperor. These great hits were brought to you by archaeology and they will replay and resonate throughout the ages, long after transient culture such as rock'n'roll or hip hop has been lost to the silence of time.

By the time archaeology came to Bermuda, it was already an old profession in other parts of the world. Some early work on shipwrecks was attempted on an archaeological basis, but the practice died out and many sites were simply salvaged. This means that the sites were not excavated by archaeological methods, nor were they recorded by those methods. Above all else, archaeology must strive to translate the physical remains of the past into an archive of records, which becomes the history of that place or monument. That translation is fundamental to archaeology, for the excavation of a site destroys it, so without the archaeology record, an irrevocable hole is created in human history. In like manner, the Taliban blew a gaping crater in world heritage with their destruction of the great statues of Buddha in Afghanistan.

In the early 1980s, the Maritime Museum engaged Dr. Gordon Watts and other professional archaeologists to examine Bermuda shipwrecks. Working with Dr. Marley Brown, the National Trust began its own archaeological programmes for the examination of St. George's and historic properties, such as "Springfield" in Somerset. The National Parks Commission has sanctioned the investigation of fortifications on parklands since the late 1980s. Many university field schools have assisted Bermuda in recovering its archaeological heritage and many local students have taken part in such scientific exercises.

After the "dig" is over, there is an eternity of preservation and conservation of artifacts found and of the records created. This is the role of museums, which are the repositories of such heritage. A number

The temporary exhibit room at Masterworks and inset, two artifacts recovered from the wreck of the **Sea Venture**

of Bermudians have now chosen careers in these various aspects of the archaeological discipline, which are outlined in the archaeology exhibit at Masterworks. Just as some of the artists of Masterworks paintings have captured a glimpse of the past for the future, archaeologists are artists with a special way of seeing into the past and preserving it for generations to come. Theirs is a noble profession: the exhibit at Masterworks shows just what it is all about.

An archaeology student excavating at State House, St. George's

Bermuda's bus stops: doomed to extinction?

Four periods of bus stops, starting with the Neolithic, progressing through Roman and Gothic traditions and ending (perhaps literally) in Plastic Age

Bermuda has several unique species of architecture, the foremost being the delightful house of local evolution. The charm of these buildings cannot be gainsaid and they were "organic architecture" centuries before Frank Lloyd Wright graced the world with his ideas and buildings. This heritage of domestic architecture is the legacy of generations of Bermudian carpenters, stonecutters and masons—most of whom were of African or mixed descents. Nonetheless, all Bermudians today should take great pride in this heritage their forebears created and take care to ensure its preservation, for more than any other facet of our cultural landscape, this architecture is what makes Bermuda Bermuda.

Another class of local architecture is the Bermuda bus stop. These little buildings are all less than 50 years old, but like many cultural species they have undergone an evolutionary process. One should remember that cars and buses were not allowed for the general populace until the year of my birth, 1946, when the Bermuda Railway was consigned to the jungles of Guyana. My arrival coincided with that of automobiles so unlike my father, I did not have to walk to school. Sometimes we went by car, but usually we rode our bikes, a death-wish habit today, which is the reason the morning roads are crowded with cars bearing children to school.

Often we went to school in buses and waited at green and white signs that said "Bus Stop." The buses were painted dark green, a legacy of war days and the Army, whose institutional vehicles were so camouflaged. The bus depot was at Crow Lane in the old train workshop, demolished some years ago to make way for the East Broadway Speedway. As passengers, you had to fend for yourself, for no thought was given to providing shelters for protection from the weather.

Then one day, some bright spark had a great idea and buses mutated into pink skins, to piggyback on the legend of Bermuda's pink sand and beaches. The bus stop signs, however, were replaced with offcuts of galvanized pipe, now painted red or blue, depending on whether you are coming or going to Hamilton. This is fine if you are not colour blind and know which colour means what.

Then another fine day, some compassionate civil servant decided that the bus populace was entitled to shelter from the rain and the first bus stop buildings appeared on the roadside. It has been a slow progression, as probably a reluctant expenditure, and shelters are still being built decades after the first. There are many varieties of this class of building and no doubt a doctorate thesis could one day be written on the subject. Here I am giving only a short term paper on this prolific subject.

The early forms of the shelters are termed "Neolithic," meaning New Stone Age, when beauty of design was not a reality. These shelters are sometimes cave-like and no more than a primitive hut in stone. Later on, they evolved into the "Roman" variety, wide open in front, with a flat lintel and sometimes built in unplastered concrete block, adding at each stop a blight on the beauty of the landscape. Then one day, the genes mutated again and the "Gothic" bus shelter emerged with two arches and a central pillar, all built in Bermuda stone. Compared to its predecessors, this form of shelter was a thing of beauty, if often surrounded by ugly concrete curbing and asphalt sidewalks. Now, the Plastic Age is upon us: un-Bermudian metal and plastic huts have appeared on the landscape in Dockyard and one hears as far away as Crawl. Is the Gothic shelter with all its beautiful attributes doomed to extinction?

The best example of the Gothic bus shelter was built opposite the Reefs. It has its arches, Bermuda stone, a bench with a back, an information sign, the standard ugly gray trashcan and lo and behold, like the star over Bethlehem, a light at night! The bench must have been put there by the hotel for the comfort of their guests and other travellers by bus. It took 40 years, but one day last year to my utter surprise, I espied a truck offloading benches at one of the stops in Sandys Parish. Yes sir, it must be to the credit of the Ministry under the Hon. Dr. Ewart Brown that people can now sit down while waiting for the bus. Halleluiah! Pews and civilization have arrived at the Bermuda bus stop.

The evolution of the Bermuda bus stop suggests—as with so many other matters—that no thought was given to the impact of the design on the environment. With any such building in a public space, the architect must answer this question positively: "Will this new edifice add or detract from the beauty of Bermuda as our home and a tourism destination?" If it is cheaper to make it ugly and non-Bermudian, the visitor will get the point and go to other destinations that certainly are cheaper if also ugly. The gray trashcans should be removed entirely, or painted pink and moved to one side of the shelter. Most visitors can still read, so let's make new signs that say "Bus stop to Hamilton," or wherever, to replace the non-verbal communication pipes in pink and blue. Make them pretty and desirable so that visitors will steal them and thus advertise Bermuda to many at little cost.

The appropriation of Portuguese Rock

On a lonely stretch of the Bermuda coast in Smith's Parish stand several small hills that form the seaward backdrop for Spittal Pond, one of the largest parks in the island. In addition to being a major park and wetland, Spittal Pond is home to a possibly significant piece of Bermuda's cultural heritage, the so-called "Spanish Rock." When we were growing up, this piece of rock was touted as an icon of the island, as to evoke mystical early days of contact by Europeans. Perhaps then as now, we loved foreign experts and so a stone called "Bermuda Rock" would have no cachet, even if Bermudians had carved it.

The rock was part of the cliff on the coast and was removed for safekeeping some years ago, being replaced by a bronze plaque. It is inscribed with letters thought to be **TF** or **RP** and the numbers **1543**. Its date of discovery is not known, but it has been variously interpreted to relate to a Spanish context. There appears, however, to be no known Spanish presence in Bermuda at that time, but 1543 was the year that a Portuguese slaver crashed onto the reefs.

There is another rock that came apparently from the coastline near Church Bay and it is inscribed with the numbers 1612. It was cut out of the cliff in order to preserve it at some time, for someone thought it to be of historical significance. Both of these rocks have a major problem of validation, for they could have been carved in 1543 and 1612, or they could have been inscribed at any date thereafter. With such inscriptions, it is well nigh impossible to date the actual carving and given the soft nature of Bermuda stone, it is surprising that these inscriptions had survived three or more centuries of a hostile climate.

Such inscriptions can be taken only at face value, with little proof that they were made in the years implied. It is possible that the Spanish Rock inscription was discovered before 1855 and was then claimed to be of Spanish derivation, as no other information was available to the contrary. In 1855, unpublished parts of the records of travels in the Americas by the historian Oviedo were finally printed and it is from that date that we have some evidence of humans at Bermuda in 1543. The late and eminent historian of the early European Americas, Professor David Quinn, wrote as follows in the first edition of the *Bermuda Journal of Archaeology and Maritime History* in 1989.

> "A Portuguese slaver, returning in ballast to Europe in 1543 crashed bow-on the reefs. Its men, including the invaluable carpenter and his tools, made their way to shore. They salvaged many materials and some food from their ship and commenced to build a pinnace, subsisting partly on large turtles. When the vessel was completed, their pilot was

A cast of the "Spanish Rock" stone on exhibit in the Azores Room at the Bermuda Maritime Museum

able to sail back to Puerto Rico where Oviedo interviewed them and told their tale in his great history, although this part was not published until 1855."

Oviedo himself had cruised by Bermuda in 1515 to drop off some pigs for use by future shipwrecked mariners, but the wind got up and he took off. He remarked on the large number of birds on the island. In 1527, Fernando Camelo, a Portuguese, was authorized by the King of Spain to settle Bermuda, but he disappeared. Oviedo in 1535 and 1537 said the Bermudas should be occupied by the Spanish to help protect their sea route to Europe against the French. In 1538 Captain Bartolomé Carreño spent 25 days here and reported on the good harbours at the east end and in the Great Sound, but nothing further came of his survey.

As far as we can tell, the next people on the island were the seamen from the wrecked Portuguese slaver in 1543 and they would have something of the same experience in 1556 by shipwrecked Frenchmen. "They found the going to be so hard and difficult, both because of the rocks and great quantity of mould (since this island is uninhabited and never visited), and because of the woods, brambles and thorns, so that they were forced to cut up their hats to put them on their feet as soles, because their shoes were all ripped and torn. In the evenings they slept beneath the tress, lighting fires to warm themselves, the light of which attract many birds which then threw themselves into it." The men ate the cahows, as the birds probably were, and drank liquor they made from palmettos.

Dr. Clarence Maxwell has noted that one scholar has interpreted the inscriptions on the Spittal Pond rock as the date 1543, a Cross (✢) for the Portuguese Order of Christ and RP meaning *Rex Portugualiae*, the King of Portugal. If that is so, coupled with the known presence of such nationals on Bermuda in 1543, it is perhaps time for the stone to be re-named "Portuguese Rock."

It is possible that it was called Spanish Rock as part of the long prevailing prejudice against the Portuguese, Bermudian and otherwise, but that assertion would depend upon the date of its naming. The Portuguese that now form a significant part of the local community only arrived here after 1849. Discrimination against newcomers was such that of all immigrant groups, only the Portuguese in the post-war period were not allowed to bring their wives or families with them when working here. There is also what some might consider to be ethnic cleansing of Portuguese work permit holders some years ago in the period leading up to the first granting of long-term resident papers.

Based on present evidence, renaming the stone as "Portuguese Rock" could correct an historical error and give respect and credit to those to whom it is due.

Pickle of Trafalgar and the Atlantic slave trade

Story of the fast little ships from Bermuda: messenger of a great maritime victory and the scourge of trans-ocean slavers

The Battle of Trafalgar was a victory that resonates through the lives of all Bermudians, though its main import seems to have been missed by recent local commentators. Trafalgar ushered in a period of supremacy of the ocean seas by the British that ensured that Bermuda was never taken over by the French, Spanish or Americans. More importantly, it led to the suppression of the African slave trade by the Royal Navy. Without Trafalgar, it is likely that the trans-Atlantic commerce in human beings would have continued up to the First World War, which marked ascendancy of the United States as the top global power. That it continues today in continental Africa is something many wish to ignore, or blame on others that have nothing to do with it.

Bermuda's part in Trafalgar is a bit of an historic pickle, as much of our history is neither black nor white and the lack of professional research leaves many questions unanswered. Such is the case with the famous HMS *Pickle*, which took the news of the victory at Trafalgar on October 21, 1805 to Britain, arriving there on November 4. The following night became known as "Pickle Night" and is celebrated to this day by Warrant Officers of the Royal Navy. Whether they all get pickled on these nights that also celebrate the foiling of Guy Fawkes' attempt to blow up the Houses of Parliament is not recorded. To pickle, in nautical terms, is also to rub salt and vinegar into the wounds of seamen caused by flogging, to add further pain to punishment.

But back to our heritage pickle: was the first HMS *Pickle* a Bermuda vessel, as most say but few, if any, publish hard facts of archival evidence? The late Dr. Jack Arnell dived into this swamp and

was of the view that it was not. More recently, local historian Edwin Mortimer has looked into the matter and some more facts seem to emerge, though we must await sight of archival documents that support the conclusion. Tradition has it that the vessel was built in Bermuda of cedar in or before 1799 and was called the *Sting*. The local shipping records do not record a vessel of that name at that time in these islands.

Be that as it may, this is the story of the *Pickle*, assuming she was the *Sting*. Shortly after being built, she was in the West Indies and was purchased at Curaçao in December 1800 by Vice Admiral Lord Hugh Seymour, Commander-in-Chief, Jamaica. The Admiralty paid £2,500 for a "clever, fast schooner," or cutter, with a coppered bottom. Edwin Mortimer takes up the story in a recent Trafalgar Night dinner address. "She was registered as a tender to the *Sans Pareil* on February 19, 1801. In October of that year she sailed to Portsmouth bearing the body of Lord Seymour who had died of a fever. By Admiralty order of January 4, 1802, *Sting* was renamed *Pickle*, and then taken into dock for re-caulking and re-coppering. In May 1802, Lieutenant John Richards Lapenotiere was appointed to command and she operated out of Portsmouth. Her armament and complement were changed and based at Plymouth. She operated with the Channel Fleet in the blockade of Brest through 1803 and 1804."

Admiral Lord Nelson, as he later was, was cruising in the West Indies in 1797 and would have met Admiral Seymour, whose death of yellow fever at 42, was the premature end that met many British military personnel in Bermuda and the West Indies in the 1700s and 1800s. Nelson died in a more direct military fashion, being shot on the day of his great victory at Trafalgar off the Spanish coast. Seymour's *Sting*, now the *Pickle*, the smallest and probably the fastest British vessel at Trafalgar, was elected to take the message of victory to England, but along with the Fleet, was delayed for several days by stormy weather. The *Pickle* arrived in Britain on November 4 and Captain Lapenotiere carried to news to London overland. Thus Bermuda, one of the smallest of ocean nations, was a significant actor in the greatest sea battle of the Age of Sail.

In Britain, they are having events galore over Trafalgar and a replica of the *Pickle* will be re-enacting the passage from Trafalgar. Someone in authority should see that a Bermuda flag is flying from her masthead for that journey. Back here at home, almost everyone is asleep at the wheel, which was fine in the days of sail. Britain has made this into a

Photo courtesy of Colin Selley

The third Pickle *off Bermuda in a painting by Deryck Foster*

EDWARD HARRIS

The third Pickle *in night battle with slaver* Boladora *in 1829. Inset, a replica of the first* Pickle *at Gloucester Docks in 2005*

major tourist event, with all the financial spin-offs imaginable. We have issued a set of stamps, but perhaps like the *Amistad*, government could sponsor a *Pickle* visit to Bermuda. The *Pickle/Sting* was wrecked, coincidentally, three years later in 1808 near the site of Trafalgar off Cadiz.

The *Amistad* brings us to the third HMS *Pickle*, which was definitely built at Bermuda in 1827. This schooner was a little smaller than her illustrious first predecessor, the second *Pickle* being a ship captured from the French. The suppression of trans-Atlantic slavery had begun in 1807, when the British Parliament outlawed the trade and Royal Navy ships began to capture slave vessels of any nation on the high seas. The *Pickle* was a part of that maritime force to destroy the shipping capacity of the slavers.

In January 1828, *Pickle* was at Jamaica and Lieut. John Bonnemaison Bunch McHardy there assumed his commission. On June 6 the following year, he captured the 16-gun Spanish slaver, *Boladora*, with 350 slaves on board off Havana, though it outgunned his five cannon. It was a night action "after a Chase of Fourteen Hours and an Action of One Hour and Twenty Minutes within Pistol shot." This became a famous David and Goliath story and its legend survived in the mid-1900s, for the image reproduced here appeared with the story on cigarette cards, now much collected. Two years later on June 18, 1831, the *Pickle* captured the slaver *Rota*, and therefore a Bermuda-built vessel played two significant parts in the suppression of the trans-Atlantic African slave trade.

HERITAGE MATTERS

45

Doing hard labour with St. Swithun

The age of the diddleybop was growing to a close in the mid-1960s. It was time to upgrade from our Zundapps, Cyruses, Motoms and other hot bikes; evading police roadblocks with our "setups" and illegal gears was losing its gloss. My late friend, Peter Moran, was heading for the US of A and a Harley Davidson ramble through California, an experience which changed his life. I was due to go California surfing with Peter, but my American mother had other plans. My Harley was a one-way ticket to university, an experience from which, as you can tell from these articles, I never recovered. Of seven children, I was the only one that went to college, for like many Bermudian families of those times, ours was of limited means.

It is unclear if that investment paid off, for eschewing the professions that looked like hard work if profitable in the end, I determined to check out something called archaeology. So in the summer of 1967 in the Age of Peace and Love, I flew out of Bermuda on Quantas for a date with destiny, or at least St. Swithun of Winchester, the ancient capital of England before the French conquest of 1066. It was actually a date with digging, for much of archaeology is hard labour with pick and shovel, trowel and dustpan. Some 200 students from all over the world gathered each summer as volunteers to help recover the ancient history of England through archaeological excavations at Winchester. It was in these summer exercises between 1967–71 that I learned the basics of archaeology and the first place I dug was none other than the original burial spot of St. Swithun.

Settlement at Winchester began several centuries before the arrival of the Romans 70 years after the birth of Christ, when they established the town as Venta Belgarum—the marketplace of the Belgae, the prehistoric population of the area. Located about 60 miles southwest of London, Winchester was home for generations of Romans until the invasions of Attila and his friends brought about the fall of Rome and the collapse of its far-flung empire. England was one of its borderlands, for neither Scotland and Wales nor Ireland were conquered by the legions of the caesars. Civilization departed with the Romans around 410 AD and there followed several hundred years of what became known as the Dark Ages, though the legends of King Arthur and Camelot shine down the centuries. Some think that Winchester was Camelot.

Towards the end of this period, peoples of northern Europe migrated into Britain, bringing into being the Anglo-Saxons, famous to some and infamous to others. In 635, one of their kings brought Christianity to Winchester, and in 648 the first church, the Old Minster, was built. It is possible that this church was the first stone building erected in England since the departure of the Romans 200 years before. Winchester became the capital of Britain and several famous kings ruled there, including Alfred and Canute.

St. Swithun became Bishop of Winchester in 852 and died 10 years later, having performed various miracles including restoring a basket of broken eggs. By his wish, he was buried outside the west door of the Old Minister, so that "passers by might tread on his grave

A composite of Winchester excavations: A—burial spot of St. Swithun; B—an apse of the Old Minister; C—mass grave. Left, archaeologist Harris in 1970

and where the rain from the eaves might fall on it." In the fashion of the day, the bones or relics of the famous were often "translated" into a more suitable sepulcher. Apparently from the day St. Swithun was to be so removed, it rained for 40 days straight. To a warm-blooded Bermudian, that aptly describes England most of the year, but the occurrence of this biblical deluge gave rise to his fame and to the jingle related to his feast day of July 15.

St. Swithun's day, if thou dost rain, for forty days it will remain;
St. Swithun's day, if thou be fair, for forty days 'twill rain na mair.

So it was on my first days in archaeology that I was given the job of excavating the remains of St. Swithun's original burial place. Having been translated, he left not much behind, but careful excavation revealed the outline in the soil of his casket or stone coffin. It rained not at all on July 15, 1967, despite my disturbance of the saint's archaeological plot. Nor did it rain for much of the next five summers, during which much was added through archaeological research to the history of Anglo-Saxon Britain. The Anglo-Saxon world came to a grinding halt in 1066, when Normans from France invaded England.

In order to build their Winchester Cathedral of 1960s song fame, the Normans destroyed the Old Minster, which had been expanded to join the separate tower to the west, dedicated to St. Martin. The Normans "robbed out" all of the stonework of the tower including its footings. In the pit left behind, they reburied all of the bones of the Anglo Saxons found in the cemetery of the Old Minster, which was excavated for the foundations of the new cathedral. We found this mass grave with some 1,500 skulls and the body bones of a similar number of persons in the summer of 1969. It was a remarkable discovery and after years of study, the remains of what could be the Anglo Saxon ancestors of some Bermudians were buried for the third and probably last time under the bells of Winchester Cathedral.

The inimitable Dr. A. C. (Archie) Hollis Hallett with his trademark pipe

Cardy Saunders, a grandson, with the weighty magnum opus

Book worth a thousand pictures

A new book, *Bermuda under the Somers Island Company 1612–1864: Civil Records*, has but one picture and it is of its author, or more exactly, its creator, the late Dr. Archibald Cameron (Archie) Hollis Hallett. It encompasses 2,000-odd pages, most of it closely packed text that recreates the early history of Bermuda from times without photography and for which few other illustrations exist. It is the most monumental piece of scholarship ever to be produced on the community history of Bermuda.

Juniperhill Press and Bermuda Maritime Museum Press have published the book with the support of 151 subscribers. I again thank the subscribers for their contribution to making this Bermuda history accessible to all, especially the outstanding support of Mrs. A. C. (Keggie) Hollis Hallett and Richard and Susan Butterfield. The publication of *Civil Records* is a part of the Maritime Museum's commemoration of the 500th anniversary of the discovery of the island by Juan de Bermúdez in 1505.

The evolution of this *magnum opus* rested in the mind of Dr. Hallett, a Bermudian of distinction as a physicist and educator. After his return home to Bermuda in 1977, Archie determined that a fuller notice of the early history of Bermuda was needed. After reviewing existing histories, in particular the *Memorials* of Governor Major-General John Henry Lefroy from the 1870s, he found them to the useful, but "historians now are seeking to probe more into details, and particularly into such subjects as slavery, the interaction between the races, land transfers, administration of justice, migration of settlers to and from Bermuda, and other topics for which the collection of selections chosen by Lefroy are not adequate."

The selections that Governor Lefroy had drawn on for his two-volume study came from the "Colonial Records" that had survived at Bermuda. The originals of most of the CR documents had been in London at the offices of the Bermuda Company, but those papers vanished after legal proceedings that led to the dissolution of the Company in the mid-1680s. Of the Bermuda documents, Lefroy selected about one-third for publication in his *Memorials*. Upon his retirement as the president of the Bermuda College in 1992, Dr. Hallett decided to bring the other two-thirds to the light of modern day "in the hope that by making the records which were omitted by Lefroy more widely available, further studies into detailed aspects of Bermuda's early history under the Bermuda Company may be promoted and

Mrs. A. C. (Keggie) Hollis Hallett

facilitated." The creation of *Civil Records* was a 10-year labour of Herculean proportions. Many who visited the Bermuda Archives over those years will remember the sight of Dr. Hallett bent over yet another barely legible manuscript. Each page was painstakingly transcribed by hand word for word, sentence by sentence and paragraph by paragraph. Many were the gaps in the documents caused by the predations of cockroaches, dampness and other indicators of neglect over the centuries. Dr. Hallett suggests interpretations of the missing fragments through his intimate knowledge of Bermuda's 17th-century history and understanding of the machinations of our forebears.

As the magnum opus was finally brought to life, Dr. Hallett's was slipping away and the last year of both was underpinned by the devotion of his wife, Keggie, who had been his partner in the production of much of Bermuda's genealogical history since 1977. *Civil Records* was to be his last offering of "meticulously researched works on Bermuda's early history and people that may be found in libraries worldwide." As perhaps only book-lovers can appreciate, Archie would have loved to live to hold the published work in his hands. This was not to be and he died on October 6, 2003, a great loss to his family and to scholarship in Bermuda.

The three volumes of *Civil Records* contain the official records of the 21 governors of the Bermuda Company from 1612 to 1684. The Orders and Constitutions of 1622 are indicative of the administration of the island. Many items of a individual nature are included, such as conveyances of land, estate settlements, bills of exchange, notes on Indians and slaves, bonds, trade and commerce, whale-fishing and cedar and early conservation methods. Wills, apprentice and indentured servants papers, accounts and debts, protests and proclamations and receipts, releases and acquittances are also accounted for.

The *Civil Records* in book form was presented to the subscribers on April 22, 2005 at the Commissioner's House at the Maritime Museum, where Dr. Hallett was a trustee for many years. Keggie and their three children, James, William and Mary, and a grandson, Cardy, were in attendance. At the suggestion of Mr. Tucker Hall, a CD of the book was included with the publication. The searchable disk greatly amplifies the usefulness of the book to all. In the absence of pictures, each said to be worth a thousand words, Dr. Archie Hallett has given us a book of text that is worth a thousand pictures and insights into the early decades of Bermuda: read it and be enlightened.

Logging in ... long before the Internet

The languages of the Internet and the sea have much in common, partly because the Internet is a word-hungry technology which has usurped many ordinary words and given them new meaning. Mice are now indispensable companions of the computer literate, who would love not the real thing. What the sailors of old would make of navigating the Net is anyone's guess. They would probably be immediate converts, for sailing ships often represented the highest technology of a country.

When we log in to the Internet, we are harking back to the days when the logbook was a vital feature of the bridge of a ship. Logging in to the Internet provides an audit trail of its usage, as the logbook of a ship provides the same for its voyages. An exhibit on logbooks and journals has opened at the Commissioner's House, with examples from the Fay & Geoffrey Elliott Collection of 19th-century Bermuda artwork held at the Bermuda Archives. Museum officer Rosemary Jones and her crew of Linda Abend, Frances Smith and Tramaine Stovell mounted the exhibition, which is open until March 2006.

Captain Alan Brooks, MBE, RN, whose personal navigation resulted in marriage to Paulina, a Bermudian, opened the exhibition entitled *Words from the Sea*. "My 24 years in the Service were punctuated on an almost daily basis by the need to keep accurate records of the activities of our ships and men," he said. "As a young officer joining a bridge team for the first time, I came to know with stark realisation the wishes of a particularly fierce navigator who wanted the ship's log to be absolutely perfect in terms of its presentation and completion. We discovered that a ruler about the head was a sure way of focussing attention on the subject! However, while this may seem a little draconian, it served in the small scale of things to make sure that we got it right, but much more importantly in the broader scale to produce accurate contemporary records of life at sea.

"These logs were living documents and recorded almost every nuance of ship's life—its course, speed, the weather, the work the ship's company were doing, the mission the ship had at that time, and how it was all going. When completed, the logs were sent off to the Naval Historical Branch, where they form a rich archive of Royal Naval activity over several hundred years. They did not gather dust,

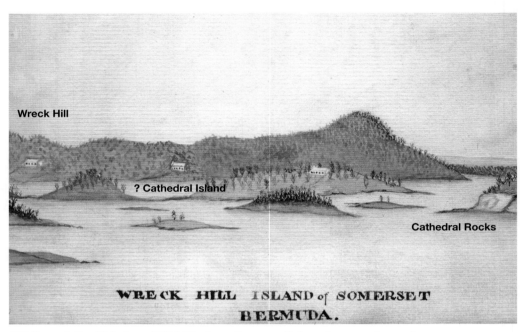

Wreck Hill

? Cathedral Island

Cathedral Rocks

WRECK HILL ISLAND of SOMERSET BERMUDA.

J.T. Brown's fanciful view of Ely's Harbour, Somerset. Below: the same view today

Channel

Cathedral Island

Ely's Harbour from Somerset Bridge

but would be used to reconstruct voyages, support legal proceedings, and provide data to naval historians."

Capt. Brooks also noted: "Journals are a slightly different kind of record and tend to be personal accounts kept by officers and ratings in the ship, because they wanted to document the course of their lives, their ship and their shipmates—a diary if you will. Nowadays, journals are kept in the main by officers under training as an exercise in developing a good written style. The subjects are invariably related to their day-to-day experiences in their ships and so journals are a source of great value to those reading after the event. In earlier days, journals were a much more widely used medium. Captains in particular would keep very accurate accounts and illustrations of their lives on board."

On such journal was kept by J.T. Brown of HMS *Tyne* on the

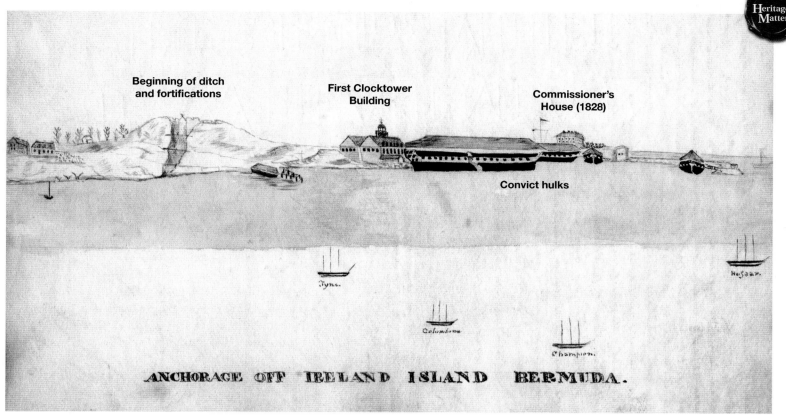

Beginning of ditch and fortifications

First Clocktower Building

Commissioner's House (1828)

Convict hulks

ANCHORAGE OFF IRELAND ISLAND BERMUDA.

The HMS Tyne *journal's depiction of Dockyard viewed from Grassy Bay. Much of today's building work had yet to be started*

From left: frontispiece of the 1828 HMS Tyne *journal; depiction of a Bermudian boat sailing before the wind; J.T. Brown's depiction of HMS* Tyne.

Fay & Geoffrey Elliott Collection, Bermuda Archives

North America and Newfoundland Station in the late 1820s. It contains information about Bermuda not otherwise recorded, including the illustrations reproduced here. That of the Dockyard is perhaps the only known "photograph" of the progress of its building by 1828, with only the original clocktower building and the Commissioner's House standing. The view of Ely's Harbour contains some artistic licence, for the little island with the house may be Whale Island and not Cathedral Island, in which instance Mr. Brown painted the scene somewhat as he wished it to be seen, not photographically as it existed.

When he arrived here, Mr. Brown had trouble with his eye and was sent to the Royal Naval Hospital. "The quarters are however very comfortable; the mosquitoes I was told were very troublesome, and moreover that there had some forty-fingered Jacks, an animal like the tarantula, seen crawling about. The rain came down in torrents and the flashers of lighting were so vivid that the whole room for a second or two seemed to be one sheet of fire. The pain in my eye was so severe that it banished all thoughts of the tarantula, and his companion forty-fingered Jack. The beds are hung with a very light sort of dimity [stout cotton cloth] to keep out the mosquitoes, which

when the rascals are all brushed out, [one] is tucked in by the nurse. The nurses are all black men, and they sleep upon rugs spread in the passage or elsewhere without undressing."

While convalescing, Brown visited the Dockyard where "the Convicts in cutting through a portion of the rock near the fortifications discovered a very large cave which I visited this forenoon. It was in the shallowest part 16 feet deep of water and had an evident ebb & flow communicating with the sea by some subterraneous passage. Into this they had lowered a boat & were in search of curiosities. One large piece whole they were hammering separated, and fell into the boat which sent them all floundering into the water. The roof of the cave is covered with stalactites some nearly a yard in length."

The Brown Journal contains a lot more information about Bermuda and its people. A cholera epidemic occurred in his time and he stated that: "The shops in Hamilton are mostly shut up, and all correspondence (daily activity) is at an end. Numbers of people have fallen victim to its fury and the people are in the greatest consternation." Nowadays the shops are shutting down for other reasons, as pronouncements on the death of tourism become a pestilence upon the land.

Why we must sustain Bermuda architecture

A couple of weeks ago, a ship bearing cement block arrived at the Dockyard and its grey cargo was offloaded on the wharf. For the next week, round the clock, trucks of all sizes thundered their way through Somerset with their loads of building blocks for the seeming insatiable Bermuda construction industry. Some of these blocks found their way off the back of the trucks to crash on the roadside, as often happens with trucks out of Dockyard carrying bags of cement. Perhaps the Police or TCD could do something about enforcing the law, if such there is, about securing the loads on trucks on public roads.

Given this latest concrete invasion, one does wonder how much more building is "sustainable development" on this small piece of heavenly rock. Sustainable development may be an unsustainable phrase, as development is a straight-line progression: it simply goes on and on consuming land and other resources, usually for one-time usage. Farming is more on the idea of what sustainable should be as it re-uses the same ground over and over. We can sustain whatever it is, if we rework, reuse and renew. The restoration of the Dockyard and Commissioner's House, for example, is good sustainable development. The replacement of the defunct Bermudiana Hotel with office blocks is the same, for the site had already been built over.

Traditions, the conceptual side of building, are eminently sustainable and no other traditional concept is more sustainable on this island than our unique vernacular architecture. The idea of a Bermuda

...or we will consign future generations to the oblivion of the universal and worthless identity of the shopping mall

house or office building can be sustained and renewed with each new generation, though one must say that many over the last decades have failed miserably to sustain the elegant traditions of Bermuda architecture.

One visiting professor some 80 years ago noted that those traditions "have developed an architecture worthy of perpetuation." Perpetuate means "to continue indefinitely; to preserve from extinction or oblivion." Sustainable or other development at the moment seems to mean to consign to oblivion much that we love about Bermuda.

John Humphreys, the professor, in his 1923 book, *Bermuda Houses*, made this statement in his preface, and it is a statement about us that should be subject itself to perpetuation:

"If Bermuda's prosperity continues to increase, it is to be hoped that the designers of new houses that appear will seek their inspiration in Bermuda's own older architecture. It is eminently appropriate to the climate and other local conditions, harmonious and in scale with its surroundings. It has a unity, charm and simplicity of an architecture that is the unaffected expression and natural outcome of environment and, from it simplicity, is entirely adaptable to the modern requirements of Bermuda."

Nowadays, we often see the totally affected expression of too much prosperity plastered across the countryside. Humphreys would be dismayed at the lack of sustained perpetuation of Bermuda's astounding architectural traditions.

With all this often in mind, it was a delight to see a few houses of old in the reproduced album, *Bermuda*, the possession of E.A. Smith in 1897, as photographed by one George Nelson. Gwen and Carl Paiva have donated the sales of this small and handsomely made book to the Masterworks Foundation, a generous gift to a worthy cause. In the album are a number of masterworks of Bermuda architecture, a couple of which are produced here; it is obtainable from C-Travel or Masterworks.

One of these is a picture of a great stone quarry, probably in Warwick, which had some of the

A young man and his cabbage patch: relaxing in more peaceful times in Bermuda

EDWARD HARRIS

Three men and the "Oldest Ruin in Bermuda." There is not a casuarina or pepper tree in sight in this scene of long ago, replete with Bermuda cedars

best limestone in the island. Two Bermudians of African or part-African descent are at work, one cutting stone, the other standing with a long chisel for digging a saw-hole behind a great slab of rock, prior to its felling for cutting into block. We have seen such pictures before, but the emphasis here is that African Bermudians were mostly responsible for the production of stone for our unique architecture. The majority, at least, of the masons who built the buildings were of the same origins. This is something of which that part of the community and their descendants should always be proud. It was back-breaking work under an inexhaustible sun that gave the island the means to produce an architectural tradition worthy, nay imperative, of perpetuation.

Another photo shows a young man with his cabbage patch and possibly his grandmother leaning in the shade of a cedar tree. A massive Bermuda chimney rises behind

Two stonecutters in a limestone quarry, most likely in Warwick Parish

her, but the property is somewhat in decay, reminding us that the island of yesteryear was not the money barrel it is today and that many families across the community were poor, were close to the land, and yet lived in sturdy Bermuda houses.

The most stunning picture in the album is described as "The Ruins of the Oldest House" and what a view into the past it is. Three men stand nearby and there is not a casuarina nor pepper tree to mar the landscape. A stand of cedars grows cheek to jowl in front of the house, but allows a gap for entry to its welcoming arms staircase. Three chimneys adorn the buildings, one for the main house, another for the cookhouse and a wonderful stubby third on an out building, probably originally the cottage for slaves, prior to Emancipation in 1834. The buildings are tucked onto the slope, away from the ridge-line and heavy weather. The ruins have all the trademarks of good and sustainable Bermudian architecture, but as far as we know, all that is left of this total gem is photograph #22 in the Smith/Paiva album.

More than any other medium, including the natural environment, architecture gives people, by subliminal education, a sense of place and identity in a changing world. If we do not sustain our architectural traditions, by restoring and renewing the old, and building afresh in the concepts of a proven and worthy past, we will consign future generations to the oblivion of the coming universal and worthless identity of the shopping mall, suburbia, gangsta rap and pants that droop around your knees, like a baby's full diapers, to name but a few of the imported ideas that can destroy Bermudian identity.

Some years ago, I saw many billboards in a foreign land that urged one to "condomise." For a brief while, I thought they were going the way of Bermuda and advocating the covering of landscape with condos, until I realised it was a sexual health warning. The Surgeon General of Bermuda should issue a warning to all that building in non-Bermudian architectural traditions is a serious health risk to present and future generations of this island.

Lightning strikes twice: theft at Dockyard

On February 17, 1975, the Queen opened the Bermuda Maritime Museum to the public, a momentous occasion that ushered in three decades of successes in making the Museum an institution of which all Bermudians, residents and visitors can take great pride. The largest project was the restoration of the Commissioner's House, which was itself opened to the public in May 2000 by then-Premier, now Dame Jennifer Smith, following major support from the government from 1999 onwards.

Upon the creation of the Museum in 1974, the government decided to transfer all the artifacts recovered from shipwrecks that were on exhibit at the Aquarium to the Museum, including objects found by E.B. (Teddy) Tucker. The government purchased a collection from Mr. Tucker in the 1960s and it included objects of intrinsic value, being of gold, silver or precious stones. The centrepiece was the "Tucker Cross," a religious relic made of gold and emeralds, the first such cross ever found, though later a number were salvaged from the wreck of the *Atocha* off Florida. A number of gold objects found their way to overseas museums; it remains a curiosity as to why they were not included in the 1960s purchase.

The day dawned and brightened on February 17, 1975 and Museum people scurried about making last preparations for the big opening. The golden goodies were transferred for the day from the Aquarium to the Queen's Exhibit Hall at the Museum and decorously laid out for the royal viewing. Minutes before the ceremony was to begin, apparently Mr. Tucker discovered that the cross bearing his name was a fake, a forgery in plastic gold and imitation green emeralds. A major piece of Bermuda heritage had been appropriated, not by smash and grab artists, but by a deliberate and criminal substitution of the real with the artificial.

The real Tucker Cross has yet to resurface. If dismembered for its gold and imperfect emeralds, it might have fetched enough cash for a week of drug addiction, but no more. Aesthetically, as an intact 16th-century artifact, it had a considerable monetary value, but only if the buyer, knowing it to be stolen goods, was willing to pay the price to keep it hidden away, for all the years ahead. We know there are people who do just that and take great pleasure out of the possession of stolen national heritage, be it paintings or any other objects of monetary worth. If it is still intact, one day the Tucker Cross will reappear, though like many Cold Case Files, it is be unlikely that the mystery of its theft and subsequent possession will ever be solved.

On or before July 12, 2005, "lightning struck twice" and three more gold objects from the Teddy Tucker collection were stolen. No substitutions were put in place, so it appears that the theft may or may not have been planned ahead. The Bermuda Police Service is investigating the matter. Whatever the outcome, the Maritime Museum has suffered a blow to its reputation as a professional institution that has otherwise so admirably cared for thousands of artifacts, a dozen Grade 1 historic buildings and an outstanding historic fort and environmental site over the last 30 years.

Now that the Commissioner's House has been finished at the modest cost of some $10 million, in addition to countless amounts of volunteer sweat equity and donations in kind, the Museum has prepared a plan for the renovation and renewal of the buildings and exhibits of the Keep Yard.

The plans call for the moving of the Tucker Treasure to another building and for it to be housed in brand new security arrangements. This will take place within a year, but unfortunately these enhancements were not in time to have saved the objects recently stolen.

The fake Tucker Cross

Gold artifacts stolen from the Maritime Museum

Over the millennia, gold has often been synonymous with greed and this has certainly been the case with buried heritage, from land sites and also from shipwrecks. A great deal of cultural heritage underwater at Bermuda was destroyed in the decades following the discovery of gold by Mr. Tucker, as salvagers and vandals ripped shipwrecks apart. The greed for gold and riches continues unabated and many think it is fair game to destroy the cultural heritage of shipwrecks, solely for private financial gain. Fortunately, we now have a new law to protect this heritage from destruction without proper archaeological work, and all artifacts from shipwrecks belong to the government and people of Bermuda.

That law can stop neither hit-and-run criminals, nor the more deliberated theft of cultural heritage from museums, galleries and historic buildings in Bermuda. Given other riotous events at Dockyard of late, it seems we have a new class of visitors to the island, persons that do not respect the law and certainly have no interest in preserving Bermuda's heritage. Our own behaviour recently, be it shootings, stabbings, or anarchy on the roads, gives one great pause in considering measures for the future protection of Bermuda heritage on public view. We are also not the law-abiding people we once were.

At the end of the day, the well planned theft of the Tucker Cross in 1975 and the recent stealing of other artifacts from the Tucker collection should also elicit one response: "Shame on you! Return this heritage to the people of Bermuda." If you know anything about these thefts, call the Police or send me an email as soon as possible.

EDWARD HARRIS

Guarding the island's last watch house

Just over Somerset Bridge on the only main road on Somerset Island heading north stands a small stone building in the shape of a Bermuda buttery. This was one of two watch houses in Somerset, the other on Cambridge Road having disappeared. It is perhaps the only watch house left intact in Bermuda of a possible 18 that may have existed from 1815 onwards, for each of the nine parishes was obliged by law to built two in their district. Built to guard the populace, it is now up to the people to guard this last memento of less violent eras, but times nonetheless that required night watchmen to keep the peace.

Under a new programme of the Ministry of the Environment, a grant was obtained to restore the Somerset Watch House. Ms. LoWayne Woolridge and her family at the property joined forces with the Bermuda National Trust, assisted by the Bermuda Maritime Museum. The road at the Watch House is extremely narrow, so the most dangerous aspect of the work was the prospect of being cleaned out by a passing vehicle.

The Watch House had tolerated almost two centuries of the Bermuda climate and the egress of destructive vegetation. Several large cracks caused by roots, the undermining of the foundations and unfinished alterations threatened the future of the structure. These matters were addressed in the restoration work. The door and windows were decayed beyond redemption and had to be replaced. The local stone building was never plastered, but only whitewashed for water-proofing, as was often the custom in Bermuda. After the stonework was repaired, the Watch House was repainted and is ready to face the future. Hopefully it will never suffer the fate of the guardhouse at Cockburn Cut Bridge in Dockyard, which was demolished in five seconds by an errant automobile some 10 years ago. It was rebuilt by the West End Development Corporation almost as it originally was, though no one guards the bridge anymore.

Watch houses have been with us at least from Roman times and the major cities of that empire had such guardhouses for patrolling the night. Watchmen were the precursors of the modern police service, which was developed in London in the 19th century. Watch houses were often erected in cemeteries and graveyards, to guard against "exhumation by doctors." In urban contexts, the watch house was a place "to keep all Beggars and Vagabonds that shall lye abide or lurk about the Towne and to give correction to such."

In 1684, the year the Bermuda Company was dissolved, the Vestry of Twickenham near London made provision for a watch house that was to be "made in ye manner of a cage with a strong lock and keye." The Somerset buttery-as-watch-house fits this bill, being no more that 10ft square and little more than a cage in stone. How much correction ever took place there is not recorded.

There is a view that watch houses in Bermuda appeared only in the early 19th century. This may be true of the more genteel parish named for Sir Edwin Sandys, one of England's leading intellectuals of the early 17th century. Dr. Henry Wilkinson, however, refers to offenders of the 1770s, who "might temporarily be locked in one of

Surveying the Watch House in Somerset. Inset: the fully-restored building

the little watch-houses with which this [St. George's] and the other parishes were provided, and in at least one district there was a room expressly provided for disorderly negroes." The reference to incarceration by colour comes from the *Journal of a Lady of Quality*, presumably not of the night. Whatever the complexion, it is clear that Bermuda had its fair share of drunks, troublemakers and felons and watch houses were an essential part of social control throughout the nine parishes.

The Somerset Watch House was included in the survey of historic buildings carried out in recent years by Margaret Lloyd and the late Rosemary Clipper with a team of National Trust volunteers. That important and monumental task is now bearing fruit as books referring to major buildings of each parish are being published by the Trust.

The Somerset Watch House is on a piece of land once owned by Joseph Watson and his wife Margaret. In 1815 they sold a small part of their land to the Somerset Vestry for the erection of a watch house, presumed to be that yet standing and now restored thanks to the individuals and bodies mentioned above. A team of archaeologists under Professor John Triggs of Wilfrid Laurier University carried out a forensic study of the little jail before the restoration, research which should be standard practice in such restoration work.

Some weeks ago, the residents of the Watch House area were awoken around 3 a.m. by a great crash resulting from a bike rider rounding Scaur Hill on the wrong side of the road, going lickety-split. Within minutes there was a traffic jam on the main road with cars lined up either way. One wonders what the watchman of old would have made of such an early morning melee and if he would ask what all those folks were doing wandering abroad at such an hour. Times and tempos change, but permanent monuments such as the Somerset Watch House remind us that civilized society lives by the unchanging tenet of the rule of law. Watch Houses, goals and prisons will always exist to confine those who think and do otherwise.

Searchlight Tattoo: blowing Bermuda's horn

One of the enduring memories of my childhood was the night we attended the Searchlight Tattoo at BAA field. The light shows, the marching bands, the police doing stunts on motorbikes, are pictures in the mind that float into the present from time to time. So it was with excitement that Majors Barrett Dill and Stephen Caton of the Bermuda Regiment hove to at the Maritime Museum to announce their plans for a Tattoo at the Dockyard on October 21 and 22 of 2005.

The word tattoo, when referring to military matters, rather than the scarification of the skin, derives from the Dutch expression *taptoe*, which meant the shutting of the tap of the beer cask at the last call in early pubs. It refers in English to a general drumming to signal to soldiers to repair to their barracks or tents at bedtime, or to sound an alarm. It is also used to name a particular type of military parade with music, drum beating and exercises, usually at night under torch-light, or in the case of Bermuda in 1957, searchlights.

The most famous of modern parades is the Edinburgh Military Tattoo, which began in 1950 and at which the Bermuda Regiment performed in 2003. The first Tattoo in Bermuda was a daytime affair in 1956, but was changed the following year into an evening event, which added considerably to the excitement of the show.

A few weeks after Majors Dill and Caton came to the Museum, Captain Sam Hummel, USMC (Ret), a member and frequent visitor, appeared on my veranda with a message on the 1957 Tattoo, which he asked be transmitted to the public.

"To the People of Bermuda: On May 16, 1957, the US Marine Corps Silent Drill Team from 8th and I Street, Washington DC, the oldest barracks of the Corps, spent an exciting week participating in the Bermuda Searchlight Tattoo. The Team performed with other special units from Bermuda, Canada and England. The Tattoo was an outstanding success from many points of view and was attended by almost everyone in Bermuda.

"One success that was not obvious at the time was the impact the Tattoo had on the Corps. After the first performances in Bermuda, it was apparent to the US contingent that the Searchlight Tattoo was significantly more popular than any performances that it had previously

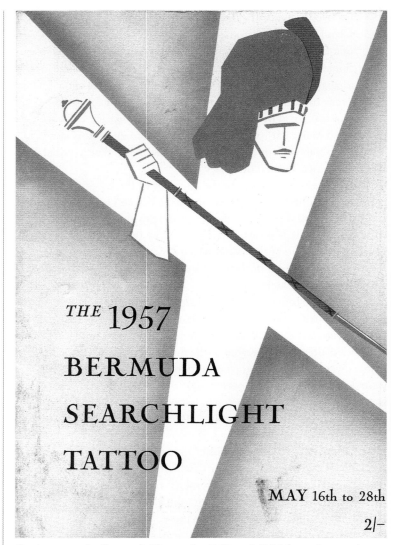

THE 1957 BERMUDA SEARCHLIGHT TATTOO

MAY 16th to 28th

2/-

Programmes for Bermuda Tattoos in 1957 and 1956 (opposite page)

participated in: it was time for some changes back home.

"In 1957, the US Marine Corps presented its Sunset Parade each Friday afternoon at the 1801 Marine barracks just blocks from the US Capitol. The Sunset Parade was initiated in 1934 and had gone through few changes over the following two decades. Despite the outstanding weekly performances of the US Marine Corps Band, Drum and Bugle Corps and Silent Drill Team, the audience was sparse in the afternoon heat of Washington summers.

"The Bermuda Tattoo changed all of that. The pageantry of this event was not lost on the officers leading the US contingent. Within days, senior officers arrived and the Tattoo was closely observed by those who could change its format after their return home.

"I cannot speak of the exact sequence of events that followed, but I can vouch for the fact that when the Drill Team arrived back in Washington, temporary metal scaffolding was already being erected at the corner of the parade fields for searchlights. In just a few days,

The US Marine Corps at Warwick Camp in 1957

the Sunset Parade was rescheduled from 5.30 to 8.30 p.m. Since that time, the Evening Parade has grown from an audience of a few spectators to an event that requires bleacher seating and reservations from Congressional Representatives or the Headquarters of the US Marine Corps. It is now one of the major weekly attractions of the City of Washington, DC.

"In 2001, a special Bicentennial Edition of the Evening Parade was produced on DVD, on the cover of which were these words: 'Performed with an elaborate lighting and spotlight system, this Parade first occurred on July 5th, 1957.' That was only about 50 days after the Bermuda Searchlight Tattoo.

Credit is given in the DVD to the fact that US Marine Corps participation first took place in Bermuda at the invitation of the organisation producing the Tattoo. It also acknowledges that after an invitation in 1958 to attend the Edinburgh Military Tattoo in Scotland, the Evening Parade became a fixed US Marine Corps tradition.

"Bermuda has contributed many special gifts to the world. This is just one of them. I want the people of Bermuda to know of their contribution to this 'fixed US Marine Corps tradition,' which has made all of us in the United States and the Corps very proud.

"I am personally grateful to the Bermuda Searchlight Tattoo because it was the reason I have come to enjoy many years of vacation in Bermuda and have come to love these beautiful islands and their people. My first visit was as a member of the US Marine Corps Silent Drill Team for that event-changing tattoo in 1957."

Sam Hummel loves Bermuda; Sam Hummel is a foreigner. Like many of our overseas friends, he shows an enduring kindness and empathy for our little island home, so far removed from the vastness of Washington DC and the American continent. Yet if the newspaper reports of the anti-foreignism and thus racism much spouted out at Cup Match are to be believed, we are increasingly returning kindness with abuse.

The US Marine Corps and other bands and foreigners have been invited to participate in the revival of the Bermuda Tattoo. This may be a time to reflect upon the revival of our noble tradition of courteousness and amity toward all our visitors—on work permits or not.

THE BERMUDA TATTOO 1956

PROGRAMME 2/-

Massed bands perform at the 2005 Bermuda Tattoo at the Maritime Museum

At the end of the world at Salt Cay

Before the world was known to be round and before Columbus sighted the Bahamas archipelago in 1492, Salt Cay in what is now the Turks and Caicos Islands was to all appearances at the end of the world. It appears so today, with its 60-odd inhabitants, derelict salt ponds or salinas, and a stunning array of decaying houses partly built in the Bermuda architecture idiom. The original Amerindians, the Arawak, might have occasionally rowed over for some sea salt, naturally dried in the salinas, but they and their successors, the Caribs, for whom the sea is named, would not have tarried long on the 2.5 square miles of low-lying sand dunes and marshes.

No-one took much notice of the place until 1681, when Bermudians intent on finding materials for trade settled in Grand Turk to rake salt there and on Salt Cay. Salt remained the main industry of the Turks and Caicos until the 1960s, when falling world prices for that essential commodity fell through the floor. On Salt Cay, the Bermudian Harriott family ran the trade, though it was nationalised in the 1950s, breaking the heart of the Harriott patriarch of the day. Unfortunately, the fashion for organic sea salt was several decades away, for it might have saved the industry on Salt Cay.

The islands were taken away from Bermudian control by the British Government and given to the Bahamas until 1848, when the inhabitants asked to be transferred to Jamaica. They remained under the charge of Kingston until 1962, when Jamaica became independent. Such a state of affairs was slated for the Turks and Caicos in 1982, but the decision was turned aside. It remains today, like Bermuda, a British Overseas Territory, of which there are 14 including such exotica as Pitcairn, Tristan da Cunha and the South Sandwich Islands. Of the 14, some 11 are islands, so the Empire is ending as it began on remote oceanic islands, Bermuda being the first island inhabited in

Examination of the graveyard illustrated the many connections by surname… though Bean of Bermuda has become Been of Grand Turk

1612 and after Jamestown, Virginia, the second British overseas settlement.

Having very little in the way of resources at home, Bermudians in the late 1600s began to look overseas for opportunities for trade. To do so, they supplied their own transport system in the form of the elegant and very fast Bermuda sloop, fitted with the Bermuda rig, thought to have been invented here, but the crucial evidence for that claim is missing. These sleek vessels, built of Bermuda cedar that was lighter but as strong as oak and impervious to the sea termite, or teredo worm, were built in the hundreds over several centuries, but little evidence survives of what they were really like, especially in the critical details of hull design.

Natural salt ponds had been seen in the Bahamas archipelago, including islands in its southern reaches, such as Salt Cay. The sea flooded low-lying areas and when the waters evaporated, natural salt crystals formed. To accelerate the process, Bermudians cut down the primæval forests to heat up Salt Cay, ushering in an early form of global warming on a very local scale. The island today reflects that devastation in its lack of mature trees of any type. Thorny acacia, prickly pear and other vegetation that like arid conditions now prevailing at Salt Cay have overtaken mahogany and other West Indies natives.

The last Harriott of Bermuda, who died a decade or so ago, used to spend half the year here and the other half at the White House, the family homestead at Salt Cay. The house has now passed to American cousins, who struggle to maintain it at long distance. Sanders Frith Brown of Bermuda has been helping them with this important task. Like many of the buildings in the Turks and Caicos, the White House, so named as it is yet whitewashed, was supposed to have been built of Bermuda stone as well as in a Bermuda style.

So it was that a decade ago with filmmaker Reimar Fiedler we

A mound of salt in the cellar of the White House

Filmmaker Reimar Fiedler at the salinas at Salt Cay

The White House at Salt Cay with a Bermuda roof

paid a visit to the Turks Islands to see and record some of our overseas heritage. Attending a church service much like that found here, an examination of the graveyard illustrated the many Bermuda connections by surname, though in some instances, the Bean of Bermuda has become the Been of Grand Turk today.

The only commodities that Bermudians could take to the Turks Islands were timber and stone; local legend here has it that the houses there were built of that stone. After a period, we came to the conclusion that this is not the case and that the stone used to erect Bermuda-like dwellings was cut on Grand Turk and is a very similar Aeolian limestone to that found here. The saltcellar of the White House, which comprises the ground floor and a basement level, is unplastered and contained no Bermuda stone whatsoever. The roof of the White House is slated as a Bermuda roof, but it could not be determined if this was Bermuda or Turks slate.

Nearby on Salt Cay is the Brown House, perhaps named for the fact that it is a timber structure, the main posts of which are untrimmed Bermuda cedar trees, still working and without a blemish or termite hole from the day they were raised in place. Elsewhere on Salt Cay, lovely historic buildings sit in general decay and several of the great salt storehouses, made of Bermuda cedar, have collapsed. One day, perhaps, research will reveal where the Bermuda stone, known to have been loaded as cargo here, went to in the West Indies.

Salt Cay remains a monument to a vital industry that once supported the Turks and Caicos and put many a pretty penny into Bermuda, which received the profits of the salt taken to Newfoundland for the salting of cod. Perhaps we should send some of that money back to assist in the restoration of a unique island at the end of the world.

The cookhouse chimney of the White House

A model history: HMS *Bermuda*

History is a matter of record, of evidence of the past preserved in documents, photographs and other archival materials. Prehistory, in archaeological terms, is the many thousands of years of human evolution for which no documents exist. Both prehistoric and historic times are joined in the study of human society by attempts to reconstruct what happened in previous eras, not only on paper but in three-dimensional imitations of ancient landscapes, town plans, house layouts and individual objects. In this venture to connect with the past, new computer games such Caesar are outstanding for their animated depiction and re-creation of times of old. One hour of playing as Caesar building a virtual empire will probably teach a student more about Roman life and history than a month in the classroom.

Before the computer, the model—"a representation in three dimensions of some projected or existing structure, or some material object, showing the proportion and arrangements of its parts"—was the main way in which the past could be re-created. In many instances, the real thing had long vanished and the model-maker, a 'reality historian,' had to compose the model from documents, photographs and other available evidence. Models are usually made in miniature and require painstaking attention to detail. An example

of one type are the Bermuda dolls' houses produced by Celia and the late Dr. Jack Arnell, much loved by visitors to the Commissioner's House.

Another outstanding model will join the exhibits at Commissioner's House, a 52-inch rendition of the last HMS *Bermuda*. Ships are one of the classic forms of models and some places like Mauritius have made a cottage industry out of the production of models of great vessels, such as HMS *Victory*. The model of HMS *Bermuda* is delightfully homegrown and has been lovingly crafted by W. Keith Hollis of Smith's Parish, otherwise known by my cousin Harold Cole of Barbados, as "The Big Onion," so named in relation to "The Little Onion," another Bermudian working in that region. Keith, now retired, had a long career with what is now the ExxonMobil Corporation. For 20 years, he served in the International Circuit and for a period was Marketing Operations Manager for the Caribbean, Mexico, Central America and three South America countries, an onion with many layers of great responsibility for a son of Bermuda.

Having seen some of Mr. Hollis' other ship and boat models, it was with great interest that I went to Knapton Hill to view his latest creation, a labour of 13 months. The model has every part of HMS *Bermuda* represented in exacting detail, showing the ship as it was in the last years of the Second World War. HMS *Bermuda* was launched on September 11, 1941 by John Brown Shipbuilders on the Clyde and was decommissioned in 1962, after a short life of 21 years.

This HMS *Bermuda* was the last of eight vessels of that name, some built here. The first was purchased in 1795, a 14-gun brig-sloop, lost the next year, as was the third, of 10 guns, launched in 1808 and wrecked in 1816. The second vessel was an 18-gun sloop, built in 1805 and sunk three years later. The fourth was a pilot boat acquired in 1813 and broken up in 1841. The fifth

HMS Bermuda *at Malta in 1943. She saw action in the Arctic and Atlantic Oceans and the Mediterranean Sea*

EDWARD HARRIS

and sixth were schooners, one bought in 1819 and foundering two years later; the other was launched in 1848 and wrecked in 1855. Thus the pilot boat lasted 28 years, but none of the others reached their ninth birthday. The seventh vessel was the great Floating Dock, towed to the Bermuda Dockyard in 1869 by HMS *Warrior, Black Prince* and *Terrible*.

HMS *Bermuda*, the eighth (C52), was the last of 11 ships of the Fiji Class of cruisers, two being sunk by enemy action, the *Fiji* in the evacuation of Crete in 1941 and the *Trinidad* on the dreaded run from Murmansk, North Russia in 1942. The others were *Ceylon, Gambia, Jamaica, Kenya, Mauritius, Newfoundland, Nigeria* and *Uganda*. The vessels were driven by steam turbine engines and could achieve a speed of 33 knots, or 39 miles per hour—twice the legal speed limit in *Bermuda*. Each ship displaced 8,000 tons, was 555 feet long, 62 feet wide, with a 16-foot draft. They mounted 12 6-inch guns in sets of three, eight 4-inch anti-aircraft guns, nine 2-pounder AA guns, as well as eight .5-inch machine guns. For additional offensive action and reconnaissance, they had six 21-inch torpedo tubes and three Walrus seaplanes. HMS *Bermuda* saw action in the Artic and Atlantic Oceans and the Mediterranean Sea, as the Honour Board at Commissioner's House in the HMS *Malabar* Room shows.

In 1945, HMS *Bermuda* was sent to the Pacific as the war drew to a close. The ship later assisted in earthquake relief for the Greek island of Zakynthos in August 1953. One official commented: "We Greeks have a long-standing tradition with the Royal Navy and it lived up to every expectation in its infallible tradition of always being the first to help."

HMS *Bermuda* made several visits to the island, at which times the people of the Bermuda presented silver objects to the ship. One of these was a large silver bell, now at the Maritime Museum, four silver bugles, trays and other items. Some of the silver disappeared after decommissioning, so if you know of its whereabouts, kindly get in touch. Two of the silver bugles were with the Bermuda Regiment, but these were exchanged with the Maritime Museum for two new ones with the regimental crest engraved, through the support of Ian Davidson, Trevor Moniz MP, and myself. The bell was sometimes used as a font for holy water in the baptism of children of the ship's complement. Perhaps it should be used in some fashion for the launch of W. Keith Hollis' magnificent re-creation of Bermuda's last Royal Navy vessel: donations of champagne gratefully accepted at Commissioner's House.

W. Keith Hollis's model of HMS Bermuda *seen from the bow*

The Honour Board of the last HMS Bermuda, *now at Bermuda Maritime Museum*

Left: W. Keith Hollis with his 52-inch model of HMS Bermuda

Jacuzzis of the Boaz Island convicts

It was a building boom that would have made the construction of the Southampton Princess or the ACE and XL buildings look like child's play yet it took place almost 200 years ago. Thirty years before, the upstart colonists in parts of North America had won a war and declared the independence of the United States, upsetting Britain's supremacy of the Western Atlantic. The Royal Navy lost all its seaports in the new country, with no presence at Bermuda to compensate for the strategic misfortune.

Someone in London put two and two together and saw that Bermuda was conveniently situated between British possessions in Canada and the West Indies. It could make a great base for the Royal Navy to keep in check the rambunctious America, later described by a British officer as a nation unwilling, if not incapable, of restraining the violent impulses of its people, which were not conducive to peace. The adversarial attitude towards the Americans continued into the early 1900s, when it was agreed that Britain and the U.S. would become allies, a bond that continues to this day.

Thirty years after the American War, Bermuda awoke one day in 1809 to the sounds of building on Ireland Island. Hammers soon rang on the heights around the Old Town to the east and the building boom began. In St. George's Parish, six great forts began to arise, from the land front at Ferry Reach with a Martello Tower to the sea front with the original Fort Cunningham. Between these grew Fort George, now Bermuda Harbour Radio, and Forts William, Albert and St. Catherine. Overlooking them from the heights of St. George's Island was the citadel or stronghold of what would become Fort Victoria.

The population of Bermuda around that time was some 10,000 souls, many, until Emancipation in August 1834, being slaves. Many of the men were employed of the new works in the first decade after 1809, but there were not enough labourers to move the work forward at an acceptable rate and so in 1823 convicts were sent to Bermuda to comprise the main workforces for the next 40 years. According to historian Clara Hollis Hallett, the Bermuda Convict Establishment was brought into being by an Order-in-Council in June 1824, the governor of the day being the Superintendent of Convicts. Hallett notes that an average of 1,000 convicts were employed daily in a multitude of tasks, including bookbinders, nurses, mat-makers, scavengers and scholars. The last presumably ran the schools that were created to educate the convicts, who were allowed time off to so improve their lot upon release. Long before "ex-pat" was coined, Bermuda would not allow the convicts to stay here upon completion of their "work permits."

The convicts, including the famous Irish nationalist John Mitchel, were housed in hulks, the name given to retired warships converted to barracks afloat. There were seven at Bermuda, with five at Dockyard and two in St. George's, for the convicts were also engaged in the building of the eastern fortifications. The English had lively names for their ships and two of the hulks were named for African animals, the *Antelope*, and the *Dromedary*— for the famous Arabian camel, of which some 700,000 run wild today in Australia. The *Coromandel*, ex-HMS *Malabar*, was another exotic named for part of the west coast of India. It arrived in 1827 with a load of timber, some being used by convicts to build the Dockyard Parsonage that year; joists found in the building were labeled "Coromandel" as a shipping consignment.

The works carried out by the convicts and local men were enormous. In addition to the fortifications at the East End, now a World Heritage Site, these workers erected every major building in the Dockyard, bar one. Ian Stranack, in his history of the Dockyard, states that up to 1834 slaves worked unfettered, while many of the convicts had to labour shackled to a ball and chain. The hills of the Dockyard were blasted away, yard by yard, and the hard limestone

No longer standing: a library photo of a hard stone bathhouse erased by Fabian

EDWARD HARRIS

Bathhouse near Lefroy House before and after Fabian. A window has been blown away and much of the front wall destroyed

Boaz Island bathhouse converted to a cookhouse

Boaz Island bathhouse covered by a 1980s promenade

carved into blocks for the great warehouses, Casemates Barracks and the Commissioner's House. The Dockyard as it largely is took 40 years to create. These outstanding historic buildings are the only ones to be built here of the very hard local limestone, still said by many to have been imported "in ballast from Britain."

By the early 1850s, the hulks were at the end of their lives and the convicts were transferred to a shore establishment at Boaz Island. It is unclear what arrangements were made earlier for personal hygiene, but at Boaz a half-dozen bathhouses were built into the water along the coast, with one nearby Lefroy House. These 'Jacuzzis' of convict days had no floors, so the convicts could sit in the water flowing through them and wash while still confined to a cell.

One of the convict bathhouses, near Magazine House, was totally demolished by Hurricane Fabian, while a splendid square one near Lefroy House was seriously damaged. The others, forming bastions

on the sea wall at the southern end of Boaz Island, were filled up and covered over to make a concrete promenade for the 1980s Boaz Island Village. While inappropriate treatment of the monuments, the walkway probably saved the bathhouses from destruction in hurricanes and storms that have followed.

At the other end of the spectrum in the 1830s, Hallett records that the Bishop of Newfoundland lunched with the Commissioner at Dockyard "where I had the opportunity of seeing his immense house … and his splendid bath, equal to one of ancient Rome." Unlike the convict who had to make do with the ocean, the Commissioner had both running fresh and salt water pumped to his bath. His marble bath survived all hurricanes except the destructive hand of man. The Maritime Museum Trustees would not sanction its replication in the 1990s, so the Museum Director has to make do with bathing in the Keep Pond with the dolphins, much like convicts of old.

Piping from Souda Bay to Sandys…

For almost 400 years, people have been immigrating to Bermuda, some of their own free will and others by force, as is the case of those who came as slaves from Africa. Others were only visiting, but had their free will negated by love and marriage in a Bermudian horse and carriage. These "immigrants by marriage" have formed a significant part of our community. Most have come to love this place as their own and in addition to their Bermudian children, they have made many contributions to the island.

In earlier times, the unsuspecting immigrant had barely stepped off the boat when he or she was collared by a Bermudian. Many were military personnel, such as my American mother, who came to work for the US Army when it was headquartered at the Castle Harbour Hotel in 1941–42. My grandfather met a similar fate in 1905 while serving with the Royal Fusiliers at Prospect Camp, marrying my Bermudian grandmother, Agnes Matilda Whitecross.

Captain Andrew Magee Sinclair is another whose military ship entered our waters six decades ago and has remained at anchor ever since, with a few furloughs overseas, Bermudian family and all. Of Scottish, Canadian and American roots, Sinclair remains one of Bermuda's finest bagpipers, with a gift for music he has handed on to one of his sons. From his early youth, one suitcase was always earmarked for the pipes, whether travelling to Souda Bay in Crete, or to the Maritime Museum at the northern tip of Sandys Parish, where he has volunteered for many years.

Recently, the "Skipper" presented his Commission Pennant for LST 32 to the Museum for display in the United States Navy Room at the Commissioner's House. Each US Navy ship flies a commissioning pennant from the moment it is brought into service until it is finally decommissioned. Capt. Sinclair took command of LST 32, *Alameda County*, from 1956 to 1958 during the Suez crisis. Wimbledon tennis champ, Lt. Gardnar Mulloy, who at 92 still meets annually with his crew from the Second World War, formerly commanded the ship.

The LST was an invention of Second World War and stands for Landing Ship, Tank, that is, a ship that could land tanks. The 1940 evacuation from Dunkirk demonstrated that large ships were needed that could deliver men and war materiel to shorelines with no docking facilities. At the Argentia Conference in August 1941, Churchill and Roosevelt agreed that the Americans should design such a vessel.

By early November 1941, John Niedermair of the US Bureau of Ships had sketched out "an awkward looking ship" that would become the design for 1,051 LSTs that were built during the Second World War. The problem he overcame was the conflict between a deep draft for ocean sailing and a shallow one for beaching the ship for offloading on an "unimproved shore." This was resolved by a large water ballast system that was filled for ocean travel and pumped out

From his early youth, one suitcase was always earmarked for the bagpipes, whether Sinclair was travelling to Crete or to our Maritime Museum

for landing the bow of the ship on the beach. The final configuration was a vessel 328 ft long, 50 ft wide in the beam, with a minimum draft of just four feet.

The LST had two bow doors and a ramp that could offload most tanks and vehicles. An elevator moved vehicles down to the ramp deck, which was well ventilated so that tanks could have their engines running as the ship hit the beach. The need for this type of vessel was extremely urgent and the building programme was given top priority. Twenty-three LSTs were commissioned by the end of 1942 and some 670 were then built at inland sites, the hulls being transported by road to seaports for fitting out. Construction of a single vessel was eventually cut to a mere 60 days, an outstanding example of American industrial output.

The LST proved to be a versatile vessel and many modifications were made. Some became hospital ships; LSTs took 41,000 men wounded on the Normandy beaches on D-Day back to Britain. Only 26 were lost to enemy action and 13 to the "friendly fire" of weather, reefs and accidents. The Korean War again proved the value of the LST, as did the Suez Crisis. Like the Merchant Navy, the great contribution of the ugly LSTs to these conflicts has often been overlooked.

When Andrew Sinclair took command of the *Alameda County* in 1956, the ship was the oldest LST in service and was transferred to the aviation arm of the US Navy. On the beach at Souda Bay in Crete, the vessel was renumbered AVB-1, for "advance aviation base," as the ship had been reconfigured to activate NATO airfields throughout the Mediterranean. Upon arriving at Souda Bay, the ship was beached, bow doors swung open and over the ramp trundled refuellers, communications vans, generators, forklifts, bomb trucks, crash trucks and all the necessaries to operate an instant airfield in the middle of nowhere.

The London *Daily Mail* in March 1956 termed the ship "Sinclair's Circus: 'Do-It-Yourself' Air Bases." The crew made a ditty about the Captain and his bagpipes.

When Sinclair's Circus sails away,
From far Cadiz to Souda Bay,
The tartan Sinclair's on display,
And a highland pipe shall lead the way.

From this one can imagine that Capt. Sinclair was an unusual CO, which one story illustrates. When visiting Souda Bay, the 6th Fleet Commander, Vice Admiral Charles Brown commented on how well the *Alameda County* was positioned on the beach. Capt. Sinclair later let slip that he used his bulldozers to bring the beach to the ship!

EDWARD HARRIS

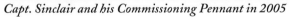

Capt. Sinclair and his Commissioning Pennant in 2005

Captain Sinclair with his pipes in a 1956 Daily Mail photo

Alameda County, on the beach at Souda Bay
Inset: Changing LST 32 to AVB-1

When priceless heritage is washed away

The recent tragedy in Louisiana, Mississippi and Alabama is a disaster of tsunamic proportions, not only for the people affected, but also for the loss of heritage, some of which is yours, for places like the French Quarter are an international legacy. As it is some 10,000 miles closer to home than the shores of Aceh, this disaster should give cause for reflection on the washing away of your heritage in New Orleans and Bermuda.

The centerpiece of Katrina's handiwork is the flooding of New Orleans and the widespread destruction of coastal towns in Mississippi and Alabama. It continues to be called a natural disaster, but it is as much manmade. The French Quarter has largely survived the flooding, as it was built on the high ground of the Mississippi River delta. The more recent parts of New Orleans were erected on lower terraces, which annually sink a few more inches below sea level. In order to have dry ground, these areas must be protected by levees and rain and wastewater has to be pumped continuously out of the settlement basin created by the levees.

The Mississippi, one of the greatest and longest rivers or the world, debouches its 1,000-mile collection of mud and silts in the Gulf of Mexico in the region of the disaster states. The river changes course at its delta every 10,000 years or so, sometimes emptying to the West and at others to the East. Many decades ago, it was prevented from making such a move that would have destroyed New Orleans and flooded of the neighbouring countryside. Billions have been spent canalising the river through the erection of dams and levees, to prevent the disaster that has now befallen New Orleans.

Each time more material is added to the levees, the town literally sinks under the weight of the earth and concrete barricades. The sinking of the town means the levees must again be raised higher. It is a vicious cycle that underlines the fact that the New Orleans disaster was as much manmade as natural, but Katrina gets the blame.

The canalising of the Mississippi has also meant that no new ground is being built in the delta, as would naturally happen, and the land-building silt is washed away in the Gulf of Mexico. Wetlands, marshes and barrier islands that are the enemy of hurricanes and tidal surges have not been allowed to develop and so hurricane tsunamis can rush unimpeded into coastal lands. Every year an area of coastline the size of Bermuda is lost to the waters of the Gulf, because it is unprotected by new growth from the Mississippi.

An archivist in Anguilla drying out hurricane-soaked documents. Below: a trolley of water-damaged Anguillan heritage

It is water, much more than wind, which causes the loss of life, property and heritage. Several years ago, Hurricane Lenny struck Anguilla and the Bermuda Maritime Museum was asked to send its conservator down to help with the devastation of its archives. Being low-lying, the heritage of Anguilla and other similar places is at high risk from flooding by hurricane waters. Here in Bermuda, our precious heritage of archives is in the basement of a government building. They will ultimately be destroyed when the building catches fire and the fire service floods the basement with water. This is one of our

Hurricane flooding in Anguilla: the low-lying island is particularly at risk from water, which typically causes more damage to heritage than wind

manmade heritage disasters waiting to happen.

What many hurricanes failed to do, we have otherwise accomplished by our own fair hands, washing away—by UNESCO declaration—world heritage in the process. Since the early 1950s, a manmade underwater tsunami has swept through the historic shipwrecks of Bermuda, leaving little in its wake. A new and just law promulgated in 2001 may stem this destructive tide. We have allowed the destruction of many historic homes and buildings, while the forts in our World Heritage Site are approaching the edge of the cliff in preservation terms.

We can have only a small inkling of the suffering being endured by the people of Louisiana, Mississippi and Alabama. Thousands have lost loved ones, their jobs, their homes and every single piece of portable and built heritage they possessed. In one coastal town, it is reported that all the historic buildings have been destroyed, along with the modern homes and business. This means that all heritage items, from the largest monuments to the smallest token of love or remembrance—especially organic things like paper and photographs—are non-history, as they have been consigned to oblivion by high winds and waters.

One Bermudian affected by Katrina—Tonisha Key-Holmes—summed it up in the *Bermuda Sun*. Hurricane Katrina, which slammed into New Orleans on Monday, has washed away all

mementos of her past life. Tonisha, 29, is a "shoe fanatic" who can't put a number on the shoes she owned. Now she has only the pair she was wearing when she left New Orleans. The numerous photo albums that provided a tangible record of her growing-up years in Bermuda and her life in New Orleans have gone as well. Several other Bermudians and their personal possessions are presently missing and, along with probably thousands of others, may have perished. The survivors will recover, but what is life without the objects of your heritage?

Ending the rule of King Sugar

The Guana Island sugar factory with molasses cisterns: ruins may soon be all that remains of the Caribbean's once-thriving sugar industry

Bermuda has a shared cultural heritage with the islands of the West Indies dating back to the discovery of our home by humans 500 years ago. A shared natural heritage existed for a million years, but who can say which was the first bird to sight the island or the first bee to alight on the blue Bermudiana? Migrating fish and turtles long transited the Gulf Stream, the largest "river" in the world, between Bermuda and the Caribbean. We also share a geological heritage, for many of the Caribbean islands are volcanic, as demonstrated so devastatingly some years ago at Montserrat.

Bermuda was the first island in the Americas and the first outside Europe to be settled by the English, when they began their worldwide colonisation with the establishment of Jamestown, Virginia, 398 years ago. Soon ships were following the Gulf Stream and the trade winds

and people filtered into the islands, but most, like Bermuda, contained little of economic interest. Then sugar, or "white gold," was introduced and that major asset took root. Sugar became King, with terrible consequences for millions of Africans south of the Sahara. The rule of King Sugar is drawing to a close, possibly to bring more ill consequences on those who have long depended on it as economic mainstay.

Bermuda does not share the heritage of sugar cultivation with the West Indies, largely by reason of geography and geology, being unsuited to its production. Its population did however eat the stuff and suffered the health consequences that remain with us to this day. It must be one of the great ironies of history that one population was enslaved to produce a commodity that addicted, maimed and killed the enslavers, through the spread of diabetes and sugar-induced health problems. White gold was the arsenic gift of enslaved Africans

EDWARD HARRIS

to Europe, though now its poison affects peoples around the globe.

As there were no sugar plantations at Bermuda, it was a privilege for several years to conduct archaeological research on such heritage in the British Virgin Islands. Working with Dr. Norman Barka of the College of William & Mary and Dr. Marley Brown of the Colonial Williamsburg Foundation, we investigated and recorded the remains of a sugar mill and factory on Guana Island, north of Tortola. The 850-acre island is largely a nature reserve, with pockets of cultural heritage, some of which is threatened by the rampant vegetation. A few flamingos walk the salt pond near the sugar factory. Their relatives were brought from Bermuda by the owners of Guana Island several decades ago, in a successful venture to repopulate the island of Anegada with such birds.

The production of sugar from cane is a very labour-intensive exercise, but by the time of its introduction into the West Indies most of the native peoples had been killed off, hence the bringing of African slaves. After the cane is cut, it is put through a mill turned by animals or wind. The cane juice is funneled into great pans and boiled until it reaches a consistency for crystallisation. At that stage, it is placed in barrels on a floor that slopes to holding cisterns. Molasses leaks out of the sugar into the cistern and is distilled into rum, thought by some to be another poisonous result of the production of white gold. After the molasses is removed, the barrels are tightened and the sugar is ready to be shipped.

The plantation on Guana Island was a part of the Quaker Experiment in the West Indies, whereby in the mid-1700s its adherents were sent there to settle and spread the faith. The experiment failed in the British Virgin Islands and all that is now to be found are the remains of the factories, great houses, slave dwellings and a few desecrated headstones at the Quaker Cemetery at Fat Hog Bay, Tortola. We excavated and recorded the Guana sugar mill and factory, the foundations of a slave house and a part of what is possibly a very rare cemetery of slaves. The object of the exercise was to enhance and explain this heritage to visitors on Guana Island, which has a very small upscale hotel.

Sugar production has continued in the West Indies but it is doomed, as subsidies from the European Union are being withdrawn, due to the mandates of the World Trade Organisation. Recently, *The Royal Gazette* reported that St. Kitts & Nevis yielded the fight this month and shuttered debt-ridden government-owned sugar mills. Other islands will follow in this cessation of an industry of four centuries, for they cannot compete on the open market with Brazil, the number-one producer, with massive amounts of cheap labour. One Jamaican grower categorically stated: "Many small island nations are not going to survive [the subsidy cuts] and you're going to have all the social consequences that go with it." The same might be said about Bermuda, substituting tourism for sugar, if the pundits are correct that the end of the rule of tourism is upon us.

All that may be left of King Sugar in the West Indies in a few years are the buildings that comprise its heritage in stone and mortar. While potentially a major tourism asset, much of this heritage is already sadly neglected. Given the shuttering up of the superpower of the region, it is possible that tourism, now the mainstay of the West Indies, may also become a thing of old, rather than the engine that supports the past and its artifacts.

Guana Island from the south with Tortola in foreground

Volunteer Tiffany Floyd excavates at the slave dwelling

Archaeologists Mark Kostro and Dr. Marley Brown on site

Getting blood from a mysterious stone

Archaeologists get blood from stones: that is their job. Archaeologists are the 'cold case' detectives for all human time before the invention of the television series. It is the task of archaeologists to discover the DNA of past events, peoples, and their cultural artifacts. The world to archaeologists is a huge Bermuda onion waiting to be peeled apart, day-by-day and layer-by-layer.

"Getting blood from a stone" is an Italian proverb of the mid-1600s related to Saint Genaro of Naples and Pouzzoli. On his saint day, the rock on which he was beheaded is said to bleed, indicating that the area is under holy protection from nearby Mt. Vesuvius, the only active volcano in Europe and one of the most dangerous in the world. The area is the home of Pozzolana, a volcanic ash that mixed with lime makes outstanding hydraulic cement, used underwater by the Romans for monuments still standing after 2,000 years.

In the later 1700s, the English translated the phrase into the less elegant culinary saying, "You can't get blood out of a turnip." Mineral or vegetable, the proverb refers to something that is extremely difficult to do. Stones cannot talk, so it becomes the expertise of the archaeologist to make them speak, to translate the solid mineral into a language of the past.

In St. George's several years ago, we found a rock sitting forlorn and out of place on the front lawn of an old military residence. The stone was out of place as it was a piece of hard Bermuda limestone

The keystone of 1846

and it had been carved into shape with symbols on its face.

We have drawn some blood out of it, for the stone itself is a giveaway. It is likely from the Dockyard where construction from 1809 onwards necessitated the blasting and excavation of thousands of tons of hard limestone. The boulders were broken down and individual lumps carved into building stones. This was the only place in Bermuda where such stone was being worked, as the Shorehills quarries at Ferry Reach probably only supplied the limekilns there. Bermudians, freemen and slaves, worked in the quarrying and from 1823, several thousand convicts were brought from England and Ireland to do the same jobs.

All of the magnificent buildings of the Dockyard, including Commissioner's House, and large parts of Forts Catherine and Cunningham were built of this wonderful limestone. So when you visit the Dockyard and someone tells you that the stone was imported, tell them that is not true. These British-designed buildings are Bermuda-built of Bermuda stone and a very significant part of our architectural patrimony.

The stone has a distinctive shape and is a voussoir, a stone from an arch. Though each wedge-shaped unit in an arch or vault is known as a voussoir, there are two specific voussoir components of an arch: the keystone and the springer. The keystone is the centre stone or masonry unit at the apex of an arch. Often decorated, embellished or exaggerated in size, no true arching action occurs until this unit is in place.

Forts Cunningham and William from the air. The original Fort William is under the large white roof, marked "A"

EDWARD HARRIS

This rock is a keystone, for it is decorated with intertwined letters and some numbers. The letters are VR and the numbers 1846, indicating that the missing arch for this stone was erected in the year 1846 in the reign of *Victoria Regina*, the last being Latin for queen. These symbols are beautifully carved in italic script. The face of the stone has a drafted margin about an inch wide, and the horizontal tooling is slightly rusticated. Several weeks would have been needed to carve this keystone and the beautiful result is probably what attracted the eye of the person who saved it.

The stone speaks loudly about a missing arch, but volumes about an entire lost fort at St. George's, the gate of which it once adorned from 1846 onwards. There are several buildings that are candidates for the lost fort. One is Fort William, known for many years at the "Gunpowder Cavern," for the upper works, possibly including an arched gate, were demolished in the 1890s when the building was roofed over to make a huge gunpowder magazine.

There is little evidence of the use of hard limestone in Fort William, so we may rule it out. Another candidate is Fort Victoria, but some crucial evidence has been lost of its 1840s composition.

The most likely candidate is the missing upper works of Fort Cunningham on Paget Island. This was designed and begun around 1820 by Captain Thomas Cunningham, RE, who went on to build the magnificent citadel overlooking the capital of Mauritius. The fort that Cunningham started was built of the hard limestone from the Dockyard and the lower level survives. In the 1870s, the upper level was entirely removed to erect the great wrought iron gunports for Rifled Muzzle Loaders, the new type of gun that replaced the cannon of earlier times. The fort was again altered in the 1890s.

The 1870s fort had an arched gateway, but its voussoirs and keystone are imitations, in that the whole is a casting in concrete, with the date of 1875. Though it looks like it, there are no individual stones. The whole gate, including the name of the fort, framed by "pilaster columns" is fake stone, cast in concrete.

Given the quality of the surviving hard limestone, much of which was uncovered in archaeological excavations in 1991, it is most likely that the stone found in St. George's town is the keystone of the original Fort Cunningham gate. It is probably the only surviving rock of the thousands that originally made up the upper, or cannon, level of the fort. Had the Maritime Museum not been granted possession of the stone by Col. David Burch, then chairman of the Bermuda Housing Corporation, it is likely that it too would have disappeared

The later 1875 concrete gate to Fort Cunningham

Fort Victoria in the old Club Med hotel. Barracks once stood in place of the swimming pool

in a dump truck, for the house, the lawn of which it adorned, was almost completed demolished by Hurricane Fabian.

The day Moore's fort went up in smoke

The year is 1619, the date October 21, the place Castle Island, and the occasion is the greeting of the new Governor, Nathaniel Butler, lately sent out from London. The party all went horribly wrong and Bermuda's only timber fort went up in smoke.

Seven years earlier, Bermuda was settled for the first time by humans; birds, turtles and a lizard or two had preceded them by a half-million years or so. After almost 400 years of depredation by humans, the surviving indigenous occupants are the cahow, some skinks, snails and a dozen or so species of vegetation. It is likely that the first settlers would be shocked at the changes to the island, which they set in train in 1612, under the first governor, Richard Moore.

One of the early settlers described Bermuda as many "small broken islands severed one from another by narrow breaches and inlets of sea, whereby are made many necessary sandy bays for the anchorage of boats…Lying thus together they become in form not much unlike a reaper's sickle, being in their whole longitude from east to west not above twenty miles English; in the latitude (where most extended) not fully two and a half…As for the soil, the innermost part of it is of two sorts, either a whitish soft rock, not much different from our English marl, or a craggy hard rock whereof lime is made."

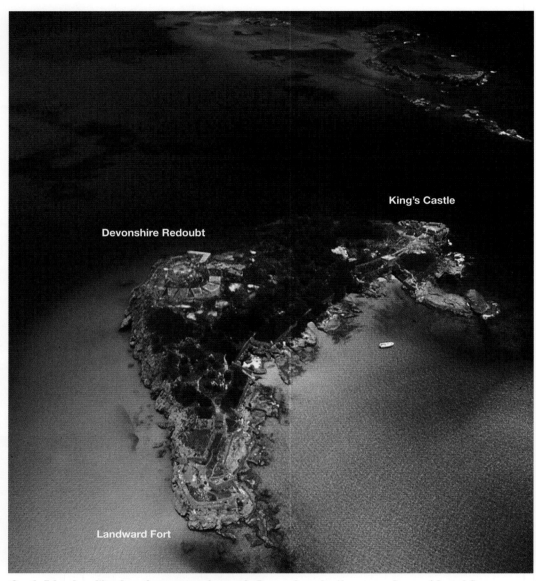

Castle Island and its three forts: scene of an early Bermuda cocktail party and an accidental fire

Therein we have the earliest allusion to the burning of stone to make lime at Bermuda, the most necessary ingredient for the building of forts, which was the first occupation of the first Bermudians. No doubt booting out some cahows and longtails from their age-old nests, Governor Moore went to town erecting fortifications at the mouths of the two important anchorages, St. George's Harbour and to the west, Castle Harbour. With one exception, these early forts were built of Bermuda stone with lime mortars and likely painted with a red limewash. The unusual fortification was the only timber fort ever constructed here and of which all traces, excepting a few archival references, have vanished.

In his history which ended in 1622, the later Governor Butler, said this in justification for writing his version of the Bermuda story: "Geography without history seemed a carcass without motion, so history without geography wandereth as a vagrant without certain habitation." On the Web, under an International Seminar on the History of the Atlantic World at Harvard University, this saying is attributed to Captain John Smith of Pocahontas fame, from his book published in 1624. Thus, it is likely to be another item Captain Smith plagiarised from Butler's history, unaware of Harvard's later rule: "Since dishonesty harms the individual, all students, and the integrity of the university community, policies on scholastic dishonesty will be strictly enforced."

The saying, whoever said it first, epitomises the role of archaeological research, for ancient sites are but geographical monuments. Many cultures did not have a written language and therefore the archaeologist, by examining their archaeological remains, seeks to create a history. Conversely, where a history exists, such in the case of Bermuda's timber fort, the archaeologist seeks to anchor that story in geographical space, to give a physical, three-dimensional reality to the time dimensions of history.

In the instance of Governor Moore's wooden fort, we have been unable to do so, although some archaeological research has been carried out at the site, now occupied by the later Devonshire Redoubt. There are only three historical references to the fort. In February 1614, Captain Domingo de Ulivarri left Santo Domingo for Spain with three ships, one of which sank south of Bermuda. On March 14, they awoke to find themselves off Castle Harbour and knowing the wishes of their King, determined to check the place out. They were dissuaded from the exercise by gunshot from "two forts about 100 paces apart; one appeared to be built of mortar and stone and the other of wood." They saw people going from one to the other wielding artillery. "There were 10 to 12 pieces in both forts." Had the forts not existed, it is possible that the ships could have taken Bermuda and we would be speaking Spanish today.

The other two references come from Governor Butler, the first from events the day after he arrived from London on "the Earl of Warwick's ship, called also the *Warwick*" on October 20, 1619. Anchored in Castle Harbour, he had some difficulties with the locals, but eventually arranged for an inspection of the fortifications on Castle Island, which he found wanting, in the usual fashion of a new broom. At the wooden fort, now termed Moore's Fort, a gunner "had made ready a piece of ordnance for his farewell, the which at his departure [Governor Butler's] he gave fire unto; this having done, and being over hasty to make after the Governor to the ship [for the party], he carelessly left his lintstock with a cole of match in it upon the platform, the which falling down upon the planks, which were of cedar and so apt to take fire, it began by little and little to kindle."

As the cocktail party (a new local tradition) was in full swing on board the *Warwick*, no-one noticed the smoke until the fort was well on fire and was utterly destroyed. Butler records that he returned two years later to Castle Island to build Devonshire Redoubt on the site of the fort that had burned down.

Devonshire Redoubt of 1621 has survived into our times and is now part of Bermuda's World Heritage Site. Captain Andrew Durnford added to its southern side in the 1790s, as the Royal Engineers took over the defence of Bermuda from the local forces after the American Revolution. Between these two works, it is likely that most traces of Governor Moore's timber fort have been destroyed, but archaeological research may yet reveal some postholes or other traces of it. Until then, Moore's Fort "wandereth as a vagrant without a certain habitation."

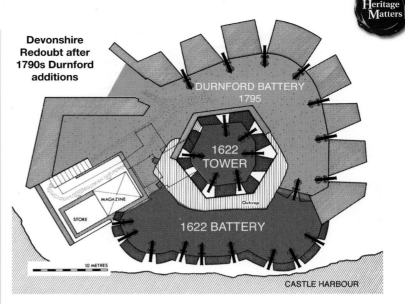

Devonshire Redoubt after 1790s Durnford additions

DURNFORD BATTERY 1795

1622 TOWER

MAGAZINE

STORE

Outcrop

1622 BATTERY

10 METRES

CASTLE HARBOUR

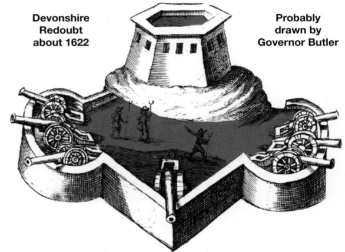

Devonshire Redoubt about 1622

Probably drawn by Governor Butler

Devonshire Redoubt in 1993

Devonshire Redoubt Tower in 2003

Slow quarrying into monumental heritage

Thirty years had passed since work began in 1809, but none of the great Dockyard buildings had yet been quarried into a legacy of monumental heritage for Bermuda. Progress then must have seemed as slow as it sometimes appears today, when comparing the images from 1838, 1858 and only yesterday.

In 1809, Ireland, Boaz and Watford Islands were sold to the British Government for the establishment of a naval base. Its purpose was to serve as a replacement for all the ports on the eastern seaboard of the new United States that were, until 1783, British possessions.

From the reaches of Maine, with all its great ship timbers, to Boston, New York, the Chesapeake and Charleston, His Majesty's Fleet had nowhere to retire for rest and repair, in between various spats with the French and now the new "Americans."

Having retained the Canadian Maritimes to the north and some of the Caribbean islands to the south, Bermuda, halfway between, was the logical—the only—geographical position for the creation of a new naval base. From there, the US could be controlled, as long as the Royal Navy ruled the sea-lanes of the Western North Atlantic.

EDWARD HARRIS

Ireland Island was chosen for the new Dockyard, after considering cutting a channel into Harrington Sound because of its protected harbour. Such a major engineering work would have been simple and inexpensive, when compared to the final cost of the western site, for all of it was composed of some of the hardest, "bastard," rock of the Walsingham formations.

Undeterred by geological intransigence, the Royal Engineers, "purveyors of technology to the Empire," began blasting soon after the erection of a few buildings on flat ground, facing the original cove of Grassy Bay. Thereafter for almost a half-century, Somerset and Spanish Point would have resounded with the sound of explosions, as the hard stone was rent into blocks for carving. The massive amount of waste rock from both exercises was economically used to make the great breakwater where cruise ships now dock.

Looking at the watercolour of 1838, the fortifications are largely completed, including (on the far left) the little fort called the Couvre Porte at the entrance to the Dockyard. The first storey of Casemates Barracks is being erected and on the far right, Commissioner's House

Three views of the Bermuda Dockyard in 1838, 1858 and 2005

has been completed for some 10 years. There is not one stone building present in the entire Dockyard itself.

In the centre of the picture is the original "Clocktower" building, which was built of timber, along with other wooden warehouses and sheds. To the left of the Clocktower is a small vessel, apparently with a derrick; this may be the boat used with the diving bell, by which method the massive stone of the dock faces were laid underwater. Several small warships and convict hulks are in the basin formed by the breakwater, the latter serving as hostels for the prisoners who did most of the construction work, from 1823 to 1862, aided for a period by Bermudian slaves and freemen.

Twenty years later, most of the major stone buildings had been erected, the masterpiece being the Great Eastern Storehouse, which yet dominates the Dockyard skyline. Another watercolour in the Fay & Geoffrey Elliott Collection indicates that the Dockyard was still void of buildings in 1847, so the monumental heritage that survives today was created in the 10 years following.

By 1858, Casemate Barracks is well in use, sporting a covered porch on two sides of its ground floor, a feature that could be reinstated. The Great Eastern Storehouse, the second clocktower building, stands to the seaward of the original, which was not demolished for another year or so. The Mast and Spar building is seen behind a composite vessel that has the mast of the days of sail, complemented by the smokestack of the coming age of steam-driven ships. A three-deck convict hulk nears the end of its life, for all the prisoners, bar one Mr. Fahy, were sent to Britain or elsewhere within the next five years. The great stone age of the Bermuda Dockyard was drawing to a close. In its last decades, stone was quarried from Moresby Playing Fields, which is why that flat sporting ground exists today.

The building of the Dockyard destroyed a great deal of the natural environment of the northern part of Ireland Island. Caves of outstanding beauty were blasted away, as even stone of pure crystal were carved into building blocks. That natural legacy was quarried into a monumental heritage, possibly the finest buildings of the Royal Navy outside Europe.

Building Dockyard destroyed a great deal of the natural environment of Ireland Island. Caves of outstanding beauty were blasted away

These buildings, the setting of the entire Dockyard, Commissioner's House, Casemate Barracks, the fortifications, and the forts defending the Dockyard at Scaur Hill and Whale Bay should have been included with the other monuments of Bermuda's World Heritage Site; this may yet happen. In the meantime, looking at the Dockyard today from the breakwater, some of the majesty of the Great Eastern Storehouse is marred by unsuitable vegetation. The fortifications, which would have withstood a cannonade from the Yankees, are being rent asunder by the dreaded casuarina.

The recent panoramic photo was created in Photoshop: the casuarinas could be scrubbed out of the picture in a few minutes. In reality, it hopefully will not take a generation to have them removed from the Dockyard and its buildings. In parts of Florida, casuarinas are illegal to plant; perhaps, as they should be seen here, their presence is considered a crime against heritage, natural and cultural.

One door closes, yet another opens...

In 1957, the date of the last major tattoo, the British Garrison left Bermuda, having been in defensive residence in the island since 1701. Prior to the latter date, we defended ourselves, though only once in 1614 were the early forts challenged. On that occasion with two Spanish warships offshore, we managed to spill the only cask of powder under the gun as it fired the one and only ball of deterrent we could muster. The Spaniards did not return fire, setting sail for Europe without tasting the delights of early St. George's Town, recorded by them as "New London."

One hundred and sixty years then passed in relative external harmony, though internal strife, some physical but mostly political, arose from time to time. In 1774, the British colonies in New England rebelled against a tax on their tea, perhaps the first consumer revolt of modern times. Tax-free tea may have become a reality in 1783 as the colonies gained independence from Britain and set in train the foundations of democratic rule, the United States becoming an icon of political ideals to many nations around the world.

Bermuda played both sides in the war and managed, in exchange for the illegal transfer of some of the governor's gunpowder to the "Americans," to maintain the flow of food to the island. Then as now, we are entirely reliant on the US for our daily bread, both the stuff we eat and the stuff we consume. Kept off the US food embargo of other British colonies, we later benefitted immeasurably by the defending of Bermuda against attack by the US.

For over a century, the British Army and the Royal Navy spent millions of pounds sterling building a great naval base and several dozen forts. The first period of forts was erected for the use of cannon, a weapon invented in the early Renaissance and lasting for three centuries as the major military tool of many early modern states. The greatest surviving monuments of this era in Bermuda are the fortifications of the Dockyard and some of the forts in St. George's Parish, the latter now World Heritage Site entities.

In the 1850s, technological advances made the cannon obsolete, along with the floating forts that were the great warships of the days of sail. The new guns that came into being at that time were called Rifled Breech Loaders and later on Rifled Muzzle Loaders. Bermuda has over 40 of these weapons, one of the largest collections in the world, ranging from guns of a half-ton firing 6-pound projectiles to 38-ton RMLS lobbing shells over 800 pounds in weight.

The new type of gun required new forms of fortifications and the building boom of the 1820–40s was repeated in the 1860s and 1870s. This time it

Fort Langton Gate as built, and its demolition in 1984. The archway was rescued

Reconstructed entrance at Bermuda Maritime Museum with mason Dennis Butterfield in wicket gate

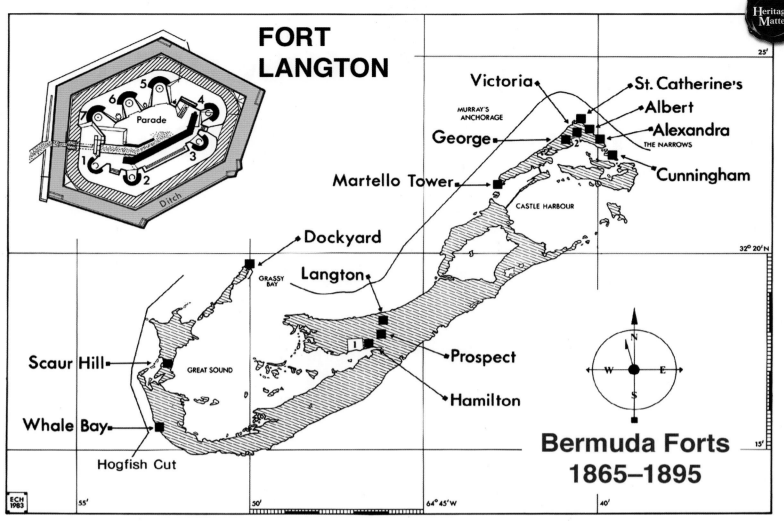

FORT LANGTON

Bermuda Forts 1865–1895

A chart of Bermuda forts of the RML era. Below: the reconstructed Fort Langton gate next to Commissioner's House

extended into the centre of Bermuda, with the building of three major works called the Prospect Position, comprising Forts Langton, Prospect and Hamilton. Southampton and Sandys Parishes also benefitted as two new forts, Whale Bay and Scaur Hill, were thrown up as additional deterrents to the Americans. At the East End, Alexandra Battery was a new work, while Forts Cunningham, Albert, Catherine, Victoria and George received major renovations.

Amazingly, given the destructive proclivities of some, all of these forts survive, with the exception of Fort Langton, demolished in 1984. At that time, we understood little about the value and history of each fort, and as it transpired, Fort Langton was the least well recorded in official records. It was unknown until some time after its demise that it was unlike any other fort in Bermuda, having both coastal and landward components, each firing different types of guns.

In 1984, the sense was that one fort was the same as another and hence the preservation community acquiesced in its destruction for the expediency of a bus depot. Many Bermudian boys knew the fort only as the island's sex education centre and in the broad light of day, it was an adventure to scale the fence and learn by anthropological observation the offensive tactics of the human battleground.

At the time of the demolition, we were able to record some features of Fort Langton, recover three cannon and take away the monumental stones of its gate. This could not have been accomplished without the great assistance of a team from Island Construction Services, the management of which later donated funds for the restoration of the gate at the Maritime Museum.

The stones of the gate were pieces of carved hard local limestone, probably from the Dockyard. The keystone is dated 1881, Fort Langton being completed as it was being made obsolete by new gun technology of the early 1880s. Queen Victoria still had 20 years remaining of her long reign and her acronym, VR (*Victoria Regina*), also appears on the keystone.

We needed a gate for the courtyard to the west of Commissioner's House and the reconstruction of the Fort Langton stones served that practical purpose, while placing a major piece of military heritage on permanent exhibit. The stonework was put back together by master mason Dennis Butterfield of Sandys Parish. The magnificent wooden gates were the creation of Austin Collin Carpenter, known to us as "Guns," an outstanding historian of British artillery and maker, with his wife Jenny, of replica cannon and carriages.

This was a window, nay, a doorway, of opportunity to give Bermudians and visitors a permanent view of the fine stone carving and proud gateway that once graced a unique fortification. Fort Langton was perhaps needlessly sacrificed on the altar of progress, as we failed to appreciate that the advancement of tourism and the wellbeing of Bermuda are inexorably linked to the preservation and accessibility of the island's monumental heritage.

Reinventing Rosendale, the natural cement

Heritage is the unconscious cement that holds societies together and built-heritage would not exist without the cements, mortars and concretes that keep it whole. For thousands of years, monuments and buildings have been erected which express in stone the ideals of a community. For most of that time limestone, one of the most plentiful rocks on earth, has been an essential building stone. It is also burned to produce quicklime that is the major binding ingredient of the mortars that glue stone blocks into buildings. Stronger cements are often required and the ancient Romans found the ingredients for natural cements, the cousins of lime mortars, in the ancient ashes of the great volcanoes near Pompeii.

Without mortars and cements, we would have very little in the way of permanent heritage, even in Bermuda. The country was lucky to have supplies of soft limestone for cutting into building blocks and a harder variety to burn in limekilns, of which many survive, if unused. The Town of St. George's is a World Heritage Site, not because its people may be outstanding Bermudians, but because it has been built of stone in a special style for several hundred years. Heritage and cement outlast people and we should be reminded often that we are but short-lived trustees of the built treasures of the past.

In the early 1800s, the building of canals in Europe and North America was an industrial craze, as companies sought cheap freighting by barge for their manufactured goods from the interior to the coast for oceanic shipping. An unintended achievement of canal building was the tremendous advances in geology, as cuttings revealed details of the earth not previously viewable. Cuttings also exposed rocks of economic value.

When excavating for the Delaware & Hudson Canal at Rosendale, New York, dolomites capable of making cements rather than mortars were found. For 75 years from 1825 onwards, Rosendale supplied 50 percent of the natural cement for the rapidly expanding US, including such structures, now major heritage monuments, as the Brooklyn Bridge and Fort Jefferson in the Dry Tortugas off Key West. The name of Rosendale become synonymous with high-quality natural cement and the town today is a unique industrial site worthy of World Heritage status.

Rosendale produced an average of five million pounds of cement each year, but after the First World War, its industry fell victim to the manufacture of artificial Portland cement. Portland cement did not rely on specialised rocks for its creation and so could be made anywhere. One cement company survived at Rosendale until 1970

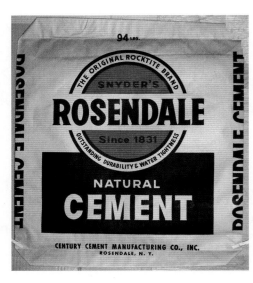

Last bag for Rosendale cement

A major contribution to the wealth and progress of the US in the 19th century

and for the next three decades Rosendale natural cement was all but forgotten.

Then a few years ago Mary Catherine Martin, an architect working on the restoration of Fort Jefferson, found that it was built with Rosendale cement, no longer obtainable. The discovery led her to Ken Uracius, a "gruff, barrel-chested mason with a Boston accent," who almost single-handed is leading the charge to reinvent Rosendale cements. Uracius believes that buildings should be restored using the same materials of their construction, but was unable to get natural cement for preservation projects.

Like lime mortars, natural cements breathe due to their porosity, without giving up any of their strength or flexibility. Portland cements breathe very little and are too inflexible to use in many contexts, including restoration of Bermuda limestone architecture. Ken cites a university building where the mortar pointing, originally natural cement, was redone in a Portland cement. Instead of moisture evaporating through the pointing, it was trapped behind it and migrated into the stonework, turning the façade of the building into a slime of mildew and mould.

His research led him to Dietrich Werner at the Century House Historical Society in Rosendale, which preserves artifacts of the natural cement industry and experiments in the making of natural cement, during which laboratory work, he almost burned down his garage. "It took me about six months to figure out how to get the rock to burn. I tried coal, but eventually bought a kiln and used electricity." He then found Edison Coatings of Connecticut, a chemical engineering firm specialising in the development and production of customised mortars and coatings for restoration work. Uracius and Michael Edison have now started to produce Rosendale cement on a limited scale for restoration purposes.

It was a privilege to visit some of the old mines at Rosendale with Uracius. The workings follow the strata of cement-making limestone deep into the hills. After the first 100 yards into the mine, it was pitch-black, with a steady, cool temperature of 68 degrees. The mine-shafts crisscross one another, so it is possible to fall through from one level to another, never to be heard of again. Fortunately, our flashlights held up and we reached the area where Ken is taking out stone. Water was dripping from the overlying strata that are held up only by columns of stone not quarried away and lakes have formed in what were once the floors of the mine. Before claustrophobia and sheer terror of the dark set in, we completed the tour and debouched into the pale sunlight of woods that have colonised the once open ground outside the mines.

EDWARD HARRIS

Fort Jefferson, Florida: built with Rosendale cement

The built heritage of the Rosendale works surrounds one in the place. Great banks of kilns that were fed by railways overhead rise in immense man-made cliffs and everywhere are the gaping mouths of mineshafts. It is an industrial wonderland and heritage site perhaps without parallel in the US, but like so many worthy monuments, it is being subsumed and destroyed by vegetation. Yet it was from here that most of the great buildings and fortifications of Victorian America took their sustenance in the form of natural cement, a major contribution to the wealth and progress of the US in the 19th century.

Hope emerges from the Rosendale mines and last year the first Natural Cement Conference was held there to promote the revival of the use of its extraordinary cement. Perhaps we might take a cue from Ken Uracius and revive some Bermuda limekilns. Lime mortars are the appropriate and natural materials with which our historic architecture should be restored. The harder, but popular Portland mortars will but cement the destruction of the very heritage we wish to save.

Two gallery levels of a Rosendale mine. Within, a maze of mineshafts crisscross one another

A bank of cement kilns

The cavernous entrance to a Rosendale mine

Last wagon of the Bermuda Railways

A train crossing Flatts Bridge, one of the 33 trestles of the Bermuda Railway. The system was financially doomed from inception and closed in 1950

J.C. "Kit" Astwood with the silver wagon

Three generations of Huntingtons: Mary, Taylor and Hilary

In 1946, Bermuda suffered three disasters in succession, having survived the 1939–45 war relatively unscathed. The effects of these misfortunes are still with us, for in that year the Bermuda Railway was facing derailment, motorcars received full licence to maraud about the countryside and yours truly was born. The vehicular pollution was quite visible on Front Street yesterday as I attempted to drive to Spanish Point and there is not a sign of the railway tracks and the tunnel under Par-La-Ville Park that is now the road of that name.

As children, we spent most summers in the cherry tree jungles on the Pitman Farm at Point Finger Road and in exploration of the old bed of the railway that is now the speeding track between the roundabouts. We were unaware that Bermuda had had two railways and that the second was still operational in St. George's Parish into the 1970s. Then a few weeks ago at the gracious home of Denise and Kit Astwood, I was shown the last railway car of these vanished transportation systems, albeit a model wagon.

The idea of a railway in Bermuda long preceded its accomplishment, like many other concepts that steamed into the reefs of our natural conservative nature. The Motor Car Act of 1908 placed a ban on private cars and public transportation remained a horse-drawn proposition. On a couple of the BELCO buildings, you may still be able to see the earlier name of the company, when it was considering getting into the people transport

business as the Bermuda Electric Light, Power & Traction Co. Ltd.

Finally in 1924 the government of the day granted a 40-year franchise to The Bermuda Railway Company to built a standard 4 ft 8$\frac{1}{2}$ ins-gauge train line from Somerset to St. George's, via Hamilton. Innumerable delays pushed the opening of the railway out to 1931. Construction and operational costs, coupled with inferior supplies of track and sleepers, financially doomed the project from its inception. As Colin Pomeroy noted in *The Bermuda Railway: Gone—But Not Forgotten*, few Bermudians invested in the system and overseas investors saw not a penny return on their thousands of pounds.

The island's topography added considerable expense in the building of 33 trestles and bridges, though the view from most was undoubtedly spectacular. There were two types of passenger coach: the "Pullman," or first-class, with its individual wicker chairs, and the third-class "toast racks," so named as the backs of the seats could be pushed over, so everyone always faced forward. The name came from the original non-pop-up electric toasters and such seats are still found in American commuter trains. The rolling stock came to Bermuda on the SS *Barbarian*, a name many may have applied to this intrusion into the sedate local landscape. A train guide informs us about Somerset: *a quiet and rural town…refreshments are served at Frith's Bar, Mangrove Bay Hotel, Summerside Hotel, The Beaches, The Cedars—* names unknown to the modern visitor.

EDWARD HARRIS

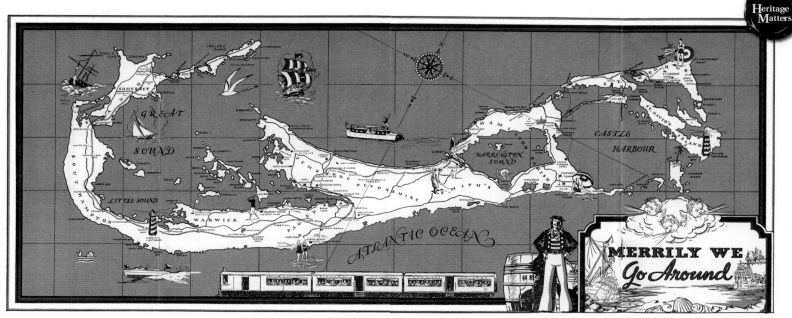

Bermuda Railway route map. Service stretched from end to end of the island—but its days were numbered after a difficult start

From the opening of the Bermuda Railway until its demise in 1947, the leading light and Chief Engineer was Harold Jennings Kitchen, otherwise known up and down the line as "The Old Man," like the captain of a ship. He was also responsible for the second Bermuda railway on Vincent Astor's property, "Ferry Reach," in St. George's Parish.

Astor inherited many millions when his father went down in 1912 on the *Titanic*. Bermudians who may not know of Vincent will know of the Waldorf Astoria, at its inception the grandest hotel in New York, the creation of his relation William Waldorf Astor. In the early 1930s, Vincent and his first wife, Helen Huntington, built their grand house, now facing the Bermuda airport, complete with a private railway that brought their guests from the main line train on the north side of Ferry Reach.

The late Herbert Bierman restored the railway in the late 1960s, when he bought the Astor estate, but all that is left are the tracks and a decayed steam engine. It was a privilege of late to visit the property with three generations of Huntingtons—Mary, an American trustee of the Bermuda Maritime Museum, her daughter Hilary and grand-daughter Taylor.

The last Bermuda railway wagon was a present to *Harold J. Kitchen, Chief Engineer and General Superintendent of All Divisions of the Ferry Reach Railway Co. from Vincent Astor*, as the inscription reads. It is a silver-plated wagon first given to *The Right Honourable Mary Caroline Countess of Erroll As a Souvenir of the Performance of Her Ladyship Of the Ceremony of Cutting the First Turf of The Cruden Branch of the Great North of Scotland Railway* in 1894. The original inscription is on the side of the wagon and Vincent Astor had the one for Kitchen engraved on the removable tray.

Vincent Astor clearly had a sense of humour. Here is an oversized gift for an undersized "performance" of cutting one turf, later given with the grandest title to the maker of one the smallest railways in the world. After he had to break up his main railway and send it to British Guiana (now Guyana), *General Superintendent* Kitchen was made head of the new division of Bermuda's public buses. He died three years later, some say of a broken heart, on December 9, 1950, my fourth birthday. So is one connected with a salient figure of our modern history.

Author's note: if anyone knows the full names of the trainmen in the photo with Harold Kitchen, kindly let me know.

| [?] Francis | Wentworth Richardson | Harold Kitchen | Maury Maybury | Jimmy Whayman | Mansfield Virgil | "Milky" Rogers | Humphrey Daniels |

Harold Kitchen and a team of Bermuda Railway trainmen

Interior of a Bermuda Railway first-class Pullman car

BERMUDA MARITIME MUSEUM PRESS